SLOW COOKING

Easy one-pot dishes for the slow cooker, oven and hob

SLOW COOKING

Easy one-pot dishes for the slow cooker, oven and hob

Photography by Elizabeth Zeschin

Antony Worrall Thompson

To all those out there who have a slow cooker and are afraid to use it... And just as importantly, to those who don't, the hope that this book provides inspiration to invest in one.

Slow Cooking
Antony Worrall Thompson

First published in Great Britain in 2011
by Mitchell Beazley
An imprint of Octopus Publishing Group Ltd,
Endeavour House, 189 Shaftesbury Avenue
London, WC2H 8JY
www.octopusbooks.co.uk

An Hachette UK company
www.hachette.co.uk

Reprinted 2011

ISBN 978 1 84533 4918
A CIP record for this book is available from the British Library

Commissioning Editor Becca Spry
Deputy Art Director and Designer Yasia Williams-Leedham
Art Direction Juliette Norsworthy
Photographer Elizabeth Zeschin
Prop Stylist Isabel De Cordova
Home Economists Sara Lewis, Lorna Brash and Nicolas Ghirlando
Project Editor Georgina Atsiaris
Copy Editor Diona Murray-Evans
Proofreader Jo Richardson
Production Peter Hunt
Index Diana LeCore

Set in Original Garamond BT and Corbel
Printed and bound in China

Note:
  Some models of slow cooker need preheating; check the manufacturer's instructions before preparing your dish. All recipes in this book can be made using a 3.5 litre (5¾ pints) working capacity slow cooker, unless otherwise stated.

Contents

Introduction

Food trends come and go and then come back again, in one big circle. Occasionally, I hope that some trends disappear forever, as with nouvelle cuisine or pretty pictures on plates, which was all the rage in the 1980s. But sadly it's back in all but name: now called molecular gastronomy, it involves a great element of science, but in essence it's pretty pictures on plates painted with tiny portions of poncey food, but this time garnished with foams and "warm jellies" instead of the 80s' favourite, kiwi fruit.

I don't blame young chefs for wanting to be inventive. I did exactly the same in my youth, but when I look back at some of the dishes in my first book, *The Small & Beautiful Cookbook*, which was published in 1984, there are some repulsive combinations that should never be repeated.

Poncey dishes are all about chefs giving customers food that the chefs want them to eat, rather than food that they, the customers, want to eat. I often wonder what these chefs eat when off duty; you can bet your bottom dollar it won't involve towers or foams. Experience tells me that chefs are partial to the occasional junk burger, a good juicy steak or a bowl of a slow-cooked classic, such as Irish stew, Lancashire hotpot or cassoulet. Mash or chips would be their favourite potatoes, and often vegetables, but certainly salad, go by the board.

I'm a fan of the Slow Food movement, which was started in Italy in 1986 to counteract the invasion of junk food that was destroying the Italians' culinary heritage. There's nothing nicer on a cold day than a bowl full of steaming food: a soup, a stew, a pot roast or a braise. Slow cooking has, of course, been around for centuries in various guises. From the bubbling cauldrons of the ancients, to the present day when many Italians, French, Spanish, Greek and Portuguese still bring casseroles of food mid-morning to the local baker, to use the turned-off bread ovens' residual heat to slow cook their dishes.

We have reached a crossroads in cooking. On the one hand is a group of chefs who are putting science back into food, using stabilizers such as xanthan gum and meat glues etc, and making their dishes very posey. And on the other, there are chefs intent on removing the spectacle of science from their food, and emphasizing instead the origins of their ingredients: by supporting the organic movement, respecting the seasonality of foods and using locally reared and slow-cooked cheaper, or should I say good-value, cuts of meat. I definitely belong to the second school. My "playground" days have long gone; now I want flavour and substance. And that's what slow cooking and the slow cooker deliver.

The slow cooker is the perfect tool for our economically straitened times, where the

restaurant customer or home cook demands value for money. It perfectly uses the cheaper cuts at the front end of the animal, which require time to bring out their best qualities. The slow cooker delivers "natural" food, as it's meant to be, with the flavours locked in. This it combines with a beautiful tenderness and such gentle cooking that the ingredients won't break up. Use it for a classic stew, delicate fish, custards, terrines, even warming punches; the slow cooker gives you so much versatility and scope.

I must own up to an initial nervousness when I started my slow cooker induction. Of course, I had cooked dishes long and slow before, on the hob and in the oven, and I was dubious about a kit that claimed to do it all for me. I was soon converted. The slow cooker's pluses are enormous: it uses less energy than a light bulb; you can walk away knowing that your food won't burn or deteriorate even if you are a little later home than planned and there are no cooking smells. It is one-pot dining at its best.

It's not magic though; there is still preparation to be done. But there is very little washing-up at the end, which can't be a bad thing. The slow cooker has been around since the 1970s, but it never really took off until a couple of years ago. Most importantly, you can have great fun with it – use this book as a guide and add or subtract ingredients as you wish. As I found out, the key is to follow a few simple rules. For example, you can take one chicken recipe in this book and create another following the same cooking times.

High on the list is getting to know your machine, as times and temperatures can vary and some models need preheating. It's also important to choose a machine that will suit the size of your family or personal needs. As a rough guide, for two you need at least a 1.5 litre (2½ pint) machine, for four a 3.5 litre (6 pint) cooker and for six or more a 5–7 litre (8¼–11⅔ pint) one is essential. The recipes in this book generally use a 3.5 litre (6 pint) or 4.5 litre (8 pint) cooker. But as a rule of thumb, buy a slow cooker that is bigger than your immediate needs, as it's a great time-saver to make larger quantities and freeze the leftovers. A good tip is to freeze the food in the slow cooker's ceramic pot, then tip out and bag the solid block – it can be returned to the pot like this for defrosting and reheating.

Most modern slow cookers have removable pots, which makes it easy to bring the food directly to the table – and helps reduce the washing-up. The slight downside is that most pots are not dishwasher-proof, as the bases are often porous and absorb water; the pot might then crack when heated. I suggest an oval-shaped slow cooker, as it accommodates terrine or custard dishes better.

So enjoy your slow cooker. I've had great fun with it as a chef, and you will too. It's an essential kitchen gadget that will give you hours of use, de-stress your life, eliminate that last-minute rush to feed the family and save you money while producing delicious food. I've outlined overleaf some rules that I learned as I became familiar with my slow cooker.

Antony Worrall Thompson

SLOW COOKER TIPS – ALL YOU NEED TO KNOW

Choosing your slow cooker

- Shape: an oval slow cooker is best. It is the most adaptable shape.
- Make sure your slow cooker has a glass lid: it enables you to monitor the cooking.
- Check the cooker's settings: most have low and high, but I would choose one that also has medium, warm and auto settings for greater flexibility.
- Size: the recipes in this book use a 3.5 litre (6 pint) or 4.5 litre (8 pint) total capacity cooker, suitable for 4–8 people. If there are only two of you, consider freezing the extra.

Preheating your slow cooker

- Some cookers require preheating – check the manufacturer's instructions and if necessary preheat your cooker before you start a recipe.
- I never preheat an empty ceramic dish; just add a little liquid first. Most slow cookers will usually take an hour to heat up, but this can be shortened by adding boiling liquid.

Cooking times and temperatures

- Always read the manufacturer's instructions carefully: times and temperatures vary from model to model.
- Dishes usually take twice as long to cook on the low setting compared with the high setting. But where recipes in this book state that a dish should be cooked on low, it is important to follow that instruction for a succulent and tender result. The following table can act as a guide for cooking times.

Oven or stove top	Low setting	High setting
15–30 minutes	4–6 hours	1½–2½ hours
30–60 minutes	6–8 hours	3–4 hours
1–5 hours	8–12 hours	4–6 hours

- The low setting: this suits meat and vegetable casseroles, chops, chicken joints, braises, soups, custard-based puddings, rice and fish.
- The high setting: this suits steamed foods and puddings, dishes that include a raising agent, patés or terrines, whole chickens and whole joints of meat.
- Remember that the timings are for advice only: a dish will not spoil if left on for longer.
- When using your slow cooker for the first few times, make notes to identify correct cooking times (you may need to decrease or increase the times). Do this by squeezing or cutting the meat with a spoon to see whether it is fully cooked and tender. Likewise, be prepared to vary the quantity of liquid used.

Preparing ingredients

- Cut both meat and vegetables to the same size for even cooking.
- For most dishes, press solids below the liquid before cooking.
- Brown meat and vegetables for a better taste. Do this on the hob, in the traditional way, before adding to your slow cooker.
- Root vegetables can take longer to cook than most cuts of meat, so arrange the vegetables around the edge and up the side of the slow cooker, where the heating elements are located.

- Soak most pulses in cold water overnight, then boil on the hob for 10 minutes before adding to the slow cooker. Pearl barley, red, Puy or green lentils don't need to be soaked.
- Add shellfish in the last 40–60 minutes.
- Do not fill the slow cooker completely: allow a gap of at least 4cm (1½in) between the food and the top. However, make sure the slow cooker is at least half full, as the heating elements are arranged around the side.
- Some vegetables don't benefit from slow cooking: these include green crisp vegetables and Asian vegetables.
- Always use good stocks where possible. The slow cooker will produce excellent stock (see pages 218–219), which can be frozen.

Pasta, rice and noodles

- Cook pasta in the traditional way to *al dente* before putting it into the slow cooker: add it in the last 15 minutes of the cooking time. Pasta goes soft if cooked from scratch in a slow cooker.
- For best results, use easy cook rice: if you are using traditional rice such as basmati, rinse until the water is clear, to prevent sticking. As a rule of thumb, use 250ml (8½fl oz) liquid for each 100g (3½oz) rice.
- Noodles do not cook well in a slow cooker.

Cooking

- Avoid lifting the lid during cooking: the condensation produces a sealed environment that, if broken, will add another 20 minutes to the cooking time.
- There is little or no evaporation: so unless the setting is on high with the lid off, you will not have to top up with water. A slow cooker recipe will generally need only half the liquid content of a traditional recipe.
- You should rarely have to stir to prevent burning and sticking: you can stir towards the end of the cooking time when on high.
- Some puddings or sauces that have a base of milk and/or cream do not cook well in a slow cooker.

Towards the end of the cooking time

- If there is too much juice at the end, turn the slow cooker to high, remove the lid and allow the excess liquid to evaporate.
- To thicken the cooking juices: fold in the cornflour paste (made following the packet's instructions) 40–60 minutes before the end of the cooking time. If you prefer to make a roux-based thickener, add the flour when browning the meat or vegetables.
- Always taste the dish at the end to check seasoning: flavours develop during cooking and it may not need as much as you think.

Safety

- The outside casing of most slow cookers gets hot: so use oven gloves.

Caring for your slow cooker

- Do not soak the ceramic pot in water when washing-up: the base is usually porous, and any absorbed water could cause it to crack when next heated.
- Never put the hot ceramic pot on a cold surface, into cold water or on the hob: it could crack.
- The glaze on the ceramic dish may become crazed after a few months: this often happens and does not affect how the cooker works.

Soups
&
sauces

Pea and ham soup

see page 30

Roasted yellow pepper soup **16**

Red lentil and white bean soup
with crisp pancetta **18**

Cauliflower and potato spice soup **19**

Baked onion soup with a Gruyère
cheese bread crust **20**

Celeriac vichyssoise **22**

Roast butternut and winter vegetable soup **24**

Chinese chicken "cure a cold" soup **25**

Seafood laksa **26**

Garbure **28**

Pea and ham soup **30**

A really useful Bolognese sauce **32**

SERVES 4 | PREP 25 MINS | COOKING 6–7 HRS | SETTING LOW

Peppers deserve more in life than just ending up as an afterthought in a salad or as a crudité dipper for a healthy option. Here's a "real" bowl of soup to make the most of peppers in season.

Roasted yellow pepper soup

4 large yellow peppers, cored, deseeded and cut into 4 lengthways

3 tbsp olive oil

40g (1½oz) butter

1 onion, finely chopped

1 garlic clove, finely chopped

1 small red chilli, deseeded and finely chopped

200g (7oz) potato, cut into 1cm (½in) dice

1 oregano sprig

750ml (1¼ pints) chicken or vegetable stock

salt and freshly ground black pepper

To garnish
croutons
grated Parmesan cheese

1. Place the pepper quarters, skin side uppermost, on the base of the grill rack and drizzle with the oil. Cook under a hot grill for 8–10 minutes until the peppers are softened and the skins have blackened bits.

2. Transfer the peppers to a plastic bag. Seal the end and allow the peppers to steam in their own heat for about 10 minutes. Peel off the skin. (Using a bag makes skinning the peppers less daunting and fiddly.)

3. Meanwhile, heat the butter in a frying pan over a gentle heat. Add the onion, garlic and chilli and sweat for about 10 minutes until softened but not browned.

4. Slice the peppers and add to the pan with any grilling juices, the potato, oregano, stock and seasoning. Bring to the boil, stirring, then tip into the slow cooker.

5. Cover and cook on low for 6–7 hours. Purée the soup in a blender until smooth and check the seasoning.

6. Ladle into bowls and serve with croutons and a little grated Parmesan.

A fiery topping
For a fiery topping to this soup, grill 6 large red chillies and 3 garlic cloves with a drizzle of olive oil until the garlic is golden and the chillies have blistered and charred. Peel, core and deseed the chillies, then blend in a mortar and pestle with the garlic, 2 tbsp balsamic vinegar, a pinch each of grated nutmeg and ground cumin and coriander, 1 tsp thyme leaves and 1 tsp oregano leaves. Season and spoon into a small jar. This will keep in the fridge for a couple of weeks. Stir into a little crème fraîche to suit your fiery or not so fiery palate.

SERVES
4

PREP
15 MINS

COOKING
7–8 HRS

SETTING
LOW

If you're into your GI diet, as I am, this is the ideal soup as long as
you keep it chunky. It has lovely deep flavours with the crisp pancetta
being the perfect partner to the earthy tastes of the lentils and beans.

Red lentil and white bean soup with crisp pancetta

3 tbsp olive oil

85g (3oz) pancetta pieces

6 thyme sprigs

2 onions, finely chopped

4 garlic cloves, crushed to a paste with
a little sea salt

1 red chilli, finely chopped

210g (7½oz) red lentils, rinsed and
drained

400g (14oz) tin chopped tomatoes

1.5 litres (2½ pints) vegetable stock

2 x 400g (14oz) tins cannellini beans,
rinsed and drained

4 slices of pancetta

salt and freshly ground black pepper

1. Heat the oil in a frying pan, add the pancetta pieces and cook over a
medium heat until starting to crisp. Add the thyme, onions, garlic and chilli
and cook for 8 minutes over a gentle heat, to soften but not colour.

2. Tip this mixture into the slow cooker, then add all the remaining
ingredients except the pancetta slices to the slow cooker. Cover and cook
on low for 7–8 hours. Check the seasoning before serving.

3. Meanwhile, in a dry non-stick pan, cook the pancetta slices over a
medium heat until the fats have been released and the pancetta is crispy
(the pancetta will continue to crisp up after it's been removed from the pan
and dried on a rack).

4. The soup can be blitzed for a smooth texture, but I prefer to serve it
chunky, topped with a slice of crisp pancetta.

A vegetarian alternative
For a vegetarian soup, just omit the pancetta and serve with some
deep-fried, thinly sliced aubergine.

SERVES 4 PREP 15 MINS COOKING 6–8 HRS SETTING LOW

It's amazing that you don't see more recipes for cauliflower soup because it has such a velvety finish, and with the addition of these wonderful spices it becomes a lovely dish for your soup library.

Cauliflower and potato spice soup

225g (8oz) onions, thinly sliced

4 garlic cloves, finely chopped

85g (3oz) unsalted butter

2 red chillies, finely sliced

1 tsp coriander seeds

pinch of yellow mustard seeds

pinch of fenugreek seeds (optional)

½ tsp cumin seeds

½ tsp freshly ground black pepper

1 tsp ground turmeric

1 tsp sweet paprika

1 tsp grated fresh ginger

225g (8oz) potatoes, diced

125g (4½oz) desiccated coconut, soaked in 300ml (½ pint) warm water for 15 minutes

850ml (1½ pints) vegetable stock

1 large cauliflower, cut into small florets

400ml (14fl oz) tin coconut milk

300ml (½ pint) double cream

salt

to garnish
coriander leaves

1. In a frying pan over a medium heat, cook the onions and garlic gently in the butter for about 6–8 minutes, until the onion has softened but not coloured.

2. Add the chillies, coriander seeds, mustard seeds, fenugreek seeds, cumin if using, black pepper, turmeric, paprika and ginger and cook for 1 minute, then stir to combine. Transfer this mixture to your slow cooker.

3. Add the potatoes, the coconut and its soaking water and the stock. Add the cauliflower and coconut milk, cover and cook on a low setting for 6–8 hours.

4. Ladle the soup into a liquidizer and blend until smooth. Pass through a fine sieve and return to the slow cooker. If too thick, thin with extra stock. Add the cream, turn the slow cooker to high and cook, uncovered, for a further 20 minutes.

5. Season to taste with salt and garnish with coriander leaves.

Slow cooker tips
If you have a stick blender, purée the soup while it is still in the slow cooker; it's quick, easy and saves on washing-up. If not, transfer the soup in batches to a liquidizer or food processor and blend until smooth, then pour back into the slow cooker to keep hot.

You can't beat a good bowl of onion soup, but to get that beautiful sweetness from the onions they need long slow cooking.

Baked onion soup with a Gruyère cheese bread crust

85g (3oz) unsalted butter

1 tbsp olive oil

1kg (2lb 4oz) Spanish onions, finely sliced

1 garlic clove, finely chopped

1 tsp soft thyme leaves

1 bay leaf

salt and freshly ground black pepper

150ml (¼ pint) red wine

1.2 litres (2 pints) beef stock

1 tsp caster sugar

8 x 2.5cm (1in) slices of toasted baguette

175g (6oz) Gruyère, grated

1. Heat 55g (2oz) of butter and the oil in a heavy-based saucepan, add the onions, garlic, thyme and bay leaf, cover with wet baking (parchment) paper and a lid and cook over a very low heat for 1 hour, until the onions have turned golden and are meltingly soft. During the cooking, stir the onions from time to time, to prevent them burning. Season to taste.

2. Add the wine, stock and sugar, then bring to the boil and simmer for 15 minutes.

3. Preheat the oven to 200°C/400°F/Gas 6.

4. If the saucepan is ovenproof (if not, transfer to an earthenware soup tureen), place the bread slices on top, sprinkle with Gruyère and then drizzle the remaining butter, melted, over the cheese. Bake in a hot oven for 15 minutes or until bubbling and golden.

To make this in a slow cooker
Heat the butter and oil in a heavy-based saucepan, add the onions, garlic, thyme and bay leaf and cook over a medium heat for 10–12 minutes, until the onions have started to soften and colour. Transfer to your slow cooker, cover with wet baking (parchment) paper and a lid and cook on low for 5–6 hours. Turn the slow cooker to high and cook, uncovered, for 20 minutes to darken the onions, stirring from time to time. Add the wine, stock, sugar and seasoning, cover and cook for 40 minutes. Then continue with step 4 above.

SERVES 4

PREP 25 MINS

COOKING 6¼–7¼ HRS

SETTING LOW

**What do you do with the knobbliest of vegetables, the celeriac?
I'm a fan of mash, but I'm also over the moon that it makes a really
interesting soup.**

Celeriac vichyssoise

2 tbsp vegetable oil

1 onion, finely chopped

1 tsp soft thyme leaves

1 bay leaf

1 garlic clove, finely chopped

450g (1lb) celeriac, cut into 1cm (½in) dice

200g (7oz) potato, cut into 1cm (½in) dice

1 tbsp lemon juice

750ml (1¼ pints) chicken or vegetable stock

salt and freshly ground black pepper

150ml (¼ pint) milk

300ml (½ pint) double cream

to garnish

few chopped chives or tiny celery leaves

1. Heat the oil in a large saucepan over a medium heat. Add the onion, thyme, bay leaf and garlic and sweat for about 10 minutes until softened but not browned.

2. Add the celeriac, potato and lemon juice, then mix in the stock and seasoning. Bring to the boil, stirring, then tip into the slow cooker pot.

3. Crumple up a large piece of wet greaseproof paper and press just beneath the surface of the stock to keep the vegetables submerged. Cover and cook on low for 6–7 hours, until the vegetables are tender. Remove the paper.

4. Purée the soup until smooth using a stick blender or transfer in batches to a blender and then return it to the slow cooker pot. Stir in the milk and half the cream. Cover and heat for 15 minutes, then ladle into bowls.

5. Swirl the remaining cream over the top and garnish with chives or tiny celery leaves.

MAKE THIS SOUP CHILLED
In the summertime this soup is delicious served chilled and garnished with ice cubes.

Slow cooker tips
Celeriac can go brown, so don't forget to add the lemon juice and keep the vegetables submerged in the liquid by adding a layer of crumpled wet greaseproof paper.

SERVES
4–6

PREP
50 MINS

COOKING
5½ HRS

SETTING
LOW &
HIGH

Squash and beans make a surprisingly good partnership – a lovely winter warmer.

Roast butternut and winter vegetable soup

2 butternut squash, peeled, deseeded
   and cut into wedges
2 onions, roughly chopped
2 carrots, roughly chopped
2 celery sticks, cut into 1cm
   (½in) dice
2 tbsp good olive oil
6 garlic cloves
1 tbsp finely chopped sage
1.5 litres (3 pints) vegetable stock
2 x 400g (14oz) tins cannellini or
   haricot beans, rinsed and drained
salt and freshly ground black pepper

for the parsley purée
2 garlic cloves, roughly chopped
1 tsp Maldon sea salt
1 bunch flat-leaf parsley, finely chopped
4 tbsp freshly grated Parmesan
4 tbsp good olive oil
juice of ½ lemon

1. Preheat the oven to 180°C/350°F/Gas 4.

2. Place the squash and the other vegetables with the olive oil on a roasting tray and roast in the oven for about 45 minutes or until the squash has softened and caramelized. Tip into your slow cooker.

3. Add the garlic and sage with the stock and half the beans, cover and cook on low for 5 hours.

4. Place the soup in a liquidizer and blend until smooth. Return to the slow cooker, add the remaining beans and turn to high. Cover and cook for 20 minutes. Season to taste.

5. For the parsley purée: blend the garlic, sea salt, parsley and Parmesan in a food processor and drizzle in the olive oil until smooth. Add lemon juice to taste.

6. Serve with 1 tsp parsley purée in each bowl of hot soup.

Also try
The parsley purée will keep for 3 days in the fridge. It's also good as a dip or folded into pasta for a quick supper.

SERVES 4 · PREP 20 MINS · COOKING 4¼ HRS · SETTING LOW & HIGH

It is always said that a Jewish mum would soothe any family ailment with a bowl of chicken soup that's "guaranteed to cure anything". I'm not so sure about that, but chicken soup definitely makes you feel better, and with chillies to add the sweat factor, maybe this will actually cure your cold!

Chinese chicken "cure a cold" soup

175g (6oz) skinless chicken thigh fillets, cut into thin strips

1 tsp grated fresh ginger

½ lemongrass stalk, tough outer leaves removed, very finely chopped

2 kaffir lime leaves, fresh or dried

2 tsp red curry paste

2 garlic cloves, finely sliced

2 red chillies, finely diced

8 baby corn cobs, halved lengthways

1 carrot, finely sliced

1.6 litres (2¾ pints) good chicken stock, nearly boiling

1 tsp Maggi seasoning (optional)

4 spring onions, finely sliced on the diagonal

8 small shiitake mushrooms, stalks removed, finely sliced

115g (4oz) mangetout, topped and tailed

115g (4oz) small broccoli florets or thinly sliced stalks

2 tbsp soy sauce

1 tbsp lime juice

salt and freshly ground black pepper

1. Place the first 10 ingredients and the Maggi seasoning, if using, into your slow cooker, cover and cook on low for 4 hours.

2. Increase the setting to high, add the spring onions, mushrooms, mangetout and broccoli and cook, uncovered, for 15 minutes. Finally, pour in the soy and lime juice, check the seasoning and serve piping hot.

Bulk up
To bulk up the soup a little more, pour boiling water over 175g (6oz) rice noodles and leave to soak for 3 minutes, drain and add to the bowls before pouring over the soup.

SERVES 4 · PREP 20 MINS · COOKING 3¼–4¼ HRS · SETTING LOW & HIGH

Good bowl food is always a treat and in this dish you have some lovely flavours with a little kick. Monkfish is the perfect slow cooker fish as it stays intact.

Seafood laksa

groundnut oil, for cooking

8 small squid, cleaned and cut into 5cm (2in) pieces

450g (1lb) monkfish fillet, skinned and cut into 5cm (2in) chunks

juice of 1 large lemon

2 medium-hot red chillies, halved and deseeded

4 garlic cloves, roughly chopped

5cm (2in) piece of fresh ginger, roughly chopped

1 tsp ground toasted coriander seeds

55g (2oz) bunch coriander (including roots)

60ml (2fl oz) sesame oil

600ml (1 pint) coconut milk

450ml (¾ pint) fish or vegetable stock

12 raw tiger prawns, peeled and deveined

175g (6oz) sugar snap peas

2 bok choi, halved

200g (7oz) dried vermicelli

60ml (2fl oz) Thai fish sauce (nam pla)

handful mint and basil leaves

3 spring onions, thinly sliced

1. Heat a griddle pan to very hot, brush with a little groundnut oil and then cook the squid for 30–45 seconds on each side until golden. Place on a plate and leave to cool.

2. Add the monkfish to the griddle and brown all over. Squeeze over the lemon juice and set aside with the squid.

3. Heat a large frying pan. Place the chillies in a food processor with the garlic, ginger, ground coriander seeds, fresh coriander and sesame oil, then blend to a coarse paste. Add this laksa paste to the heated pan and stir-fry for 1 minute, then pour in the coconut milk and stock and bring to the boil. Spoon into your slow cooker with the squid and the monkfish, then cover and cook on low for 3–4 hours.

4. Add the prawns, sugar snaps and bok choi, and cook, uncovered, on high for 15 minutes.

5. Meanwhile, place the vermicelli in a large saucepan of boiling salted water and then immediately remove from the heat. Set aside for 3–4 minutes, depending on the manufacturer's instructions, then drain and refresh under cold running water. Set aside.

6. Add the fish sauce to the slow cooker pot with half the herbs and stir gently for a few seconds.

7. Divide the cooked vermicelli between the serving bowls and ladle the seafood laksa on top, then sprinkle over the remaining mint and basil leaves and the spring onions. Serve piping hot.

Also try
Why not try octopus instead of squid, and scallops or crab instead of prawns.

SERVES 6–8 · PREP 20 MINS · SOAK OVERNIGHT · COOKING 3¾ HRS · HOB

Nothing is nicer than a bowl of this southwestern French dish on a cold day. Don't try to hurry this, the secret is in the long slow cooking until the meat is quite literally falling off the hock bone and the flavours have blended together.

Garbure

225g (8oz) white haricot beans, soaked overnight in cold water

225g (8oz) piece of salt pork belly

2 medium leeks, shredded

225g (8oz) new potatoes, washed and halved

6 celery sticks, thinly sliced

6 baby turnips

1 ham or bacon hock, soaked overnight in cold water

6 garlic cloves, finely chopped

2 thyme sprigs

2 onions, thinly sliced

2 carrots, thinly sliced

2 bay leaves

3 litres (5¼ pints) chicken stock

1 small Savoy cabbage, shredded

4 duck confit legs, meat shredded

salt and freshly ground black pepper

to garnish
roughly chopped flat-leaf parsley

1. Drain the beans and boil in unsalted water for 40 minutes. Drain and discard the cooking water. Put the beans into a large saucepan and add the pork, leeks, potatoes, celery, turnips, ham hock, garlic, thyme, onions, carrots, bay leaves and stock. Simmer for 2 hours 45 minutes, skimming off the scum from time to time, until the meat is cooked through.

2. Add the cabbage and duck confit, and simmer for a further 20 minutes.

3. Remove the pork belly and ham hock. Place the pork belly in a food processor and blend until smooth, then stir it back into the soup. Remove the meat from the ham hock and shred, then fold into the soup. Season to taste and garnish with parsley.

We've grown used to making pea soup with frozen peas – nowt wrong with that – but for real flavour the slow cooker comes into its own with the genuine article, split peas. If you can't get a ham hock from your butcher, use a small bacon joint.

Pea and ham soup

325g (11½oz) split green peas

1 tbsp rapeseed oil

1 onion, finely chopped

4 garlic cloves, finely chopped

1 tsp soft thyme leaves

2 bay leaves

1 ham hock (approximately 1kg/2lb 4oz), soaked overnight in cold water

2 medium carrots, finely diced

2 celery sticks, finely diced

1.8 litres (3 pints) chicken stock

salt and freshly ground black pepper

to garnish

120ml (4fl oz) crème fraîche or Greek yoghurt

2 tsp finely chopped mint

2 tsp finely chopped chives

1. Rinse the peas under cold water and drain.

2. In a frying pan, heat the oil over a medium heat and gently cook the onion, garlic, thyme and bay for 10 minutes, until the onion has softened but has not coloured. Spoon into your slow cooker.

3. Add all the remaining soup ingredients, except the seasoning, to the slow cooker, then cover and cook on a low heat for 8 hours, until the meat is cooked through.

4. Remove the ham hock from the cooker. Allow to cool enough to handle, then cut off and discard the rind and most of the fat. Remove the meat from the hock and coarsely chop, then stir it back into the soup. Season to taste.

5. For the garnish, combine all the ingredients. Spoon a dollop on top of each bowl of soup.

SERVES
12

PREP
30 MINS

4·5L
COOKING
10½ HRS
LARGE POT

SETTING
LOW &
HIGH

Over the past decade minced beef dishes have slipped out of favour with many people, which is a pity. This Bolognese sauce is a perfect standby for converting into any mince-type dish, such as moussaka, cannelloni, chilli con carne, lasagne, cottage pie and fillings for pancakes and jacket potatoes. It's an ideal recipe to make in big batches for the freezer.

A really useful Bolognese sauce

115g (4oz) smoked streaky bacon or pancetta, diced

up to 300ml (½ pint) good olive oil

2 onions, finely diced

2 celery sticks, finely diced

2 carrots, finely sliced

5 garlic cloves, crushed to a paste with a little sea salt

2 bay leaves

2 tsp dried oregano

1.8kg (4lb) minced beef

2 x 400g (14oz) tins chopped tomatoes

2 tbsp tomato purée

1 tbsp anchovy essence

2 tbsp Worcestershire sauce

250g (9oz) fresh chicken livers, finely chopped

1 bottle red wine

1 litre (1¾ pints) chicken, beef or lamb stock

2 tbsp basil leaves

1 tbsp fresh oregano leaves

salt and freshly ground black pepper

1. In a large frying pan, fry the bacon in 1 tbsp olive oil over a medium heat. When the bacon is crispy and has released some fat, add the onions, celery, carrots, garlic, bay leaves and dried oregano and cook until the vegetables have softened and taken on a little colour. Spoon into the slow cooker.

2. Then in the same frying pan, heat 1 tbsp olive oil and fry the mince over a high heat in small batches until browned. While the meat is frying, break up any lumps with the back of a wooden spoon. When browned, add the meat to the vegetable mix in the slow cooker.

3. Add the tinned tomatoes, tomato purée, anchovy essence, Worcestershire sauce, chicken livers, red wine and stock and stir. Cover and cook on low for 10 hours until the meat is cooked. Stir to combine.

4. Turn the cooker to high and stir in the herbs, season to taste, then cook, uncovered, for 20 minutes.

On the side

Apricot and orange chutney
see page 48

Aromatic aubergine with feta and spinach **38**

Rice with some nice spice **40**

Slow-cooked courgettes **41**

Slow-cooked fennel with tomatoes,
olives and crispy crumbs **42**

Red lentil dip **44**

Spicy braised aubergines with prunes **45**

Prosciutto-wrapped braised celery **46**

Apricot and orange chutney **48**

SERVES 4–6 · PREP 15 MINS · COOKING 5¼–6¼ HRS · SETTING LOW & HIGH

Love them or hate them, aubergines are very much part of our supermarket shelves, but they do need added flavour. This is a dip-cum-vegetable starter with loads going on and a great taste.

Aromatic aubergine with feta and spinach

1kg (2lb 4oz) aubergine

3 tbsp groundnut oil

2 tbsp finely chopped garlic

1 tbsp grated fresh ginger

8 spring onions, finely sliced

¾ tsp dried chilli flakes

5 tbsp light soy sauce

4 tbsp soft dark brown sugar

1 tbsp rice vinegar

2 tbsp mirin or dry sherry

175g (6oz) good feta cheese, diced

1 tsp sesame oil

325g (11½oz) baby spinach

1 tbsp roughly chopped coriander leaves

4 tbsp Greek yoghurt (optional)

1. Place the aubergine directly over the gas flame on your hob or under a very hot grill and cook until charred all over, turning from time to time (this gives a much smokier flavour).

2. When cool enough to handle, scrape off the charred skin and roughly chop the flesh. Add to your slow cooker.

3. Meanwhile, put the groundnut oil in a wok or frying pan over a high heat, then add the garlic, ginger, spring onions and chilli flakes and stir-fry for 30 seconds. Add the soy sauce, sugar, rice vinegar and mirin and stir to combine. Cook for 1 minute.

4. Fold into the aubergine in the slow cooker, cover and cook on low for 5–6 hours. Then turn your cooker to high and fold in the feta, sesame oil, spinach and coriander leaves. Cook, uncovered, for 15 minutes.

5. Serve with a dollop of yoghurt if you like.

SERVING SUGGESTION
Serve with raw vegetable crudités, or with long-grain rice, noodles or pitta bread.

SERVES
4

PREP
25 MINS

COOKING
3 HRS

SETTING
LOW &
HIGH

Some of my favourite meals involve a bowl of rice with loads of bits. I'm a recent convert to brown rice, as I've come to realize that white rice has been stripped of most of its goodness. This dish could act as a base for all sorts of other goodies – prawns, pork, chicken, leftovers from the Sunday roast – and it's equally delicious as a vegetarian dish.

Rice with some nice spice

2 tbsp sunflower or vegetable oil

1 onion, finely chopped

3 garlic cloves, crushed to a paste with a little sea salt

1 carrot, finely diced

1 celery stick, finely sliced

250g (9oz) easy-cook brown rice, rinsed and drained

½ tsp each garam masala, chilli powder and ground cumin, coriander and turmeric

600ml (1 pint) vegetable stock, boiling

200g (7oz) tin chopped tomatoes

200g (7oz) tin sweetcorn, drained

2 roasted peppers, from a jar, cut into small dice

2 handfuls baby spinach

25g (1oz) unsalted butter

salt and freshly ground black pepper

25g (1oz) cashew nuts, roughly chopped

1. Heat the oil in a frying pan, then add the onion, garlic, carrot and celery and cook gently for 10 minutes, until the vegetables have started to soften but haven't taken on much colour.

2. Add the rice and spices and cook for 2 minutes, stirring constantly, then tip the contents of the frying pan into your slow cooker. Pour in the stock, tomatoes and sweetcorn, cover and cook on low for 2 hours.

3. Lift the lid, fold in the peppers, then lay the spinach on the surface and dot with the butter. Increase the setting to high, cover and cook for 40 minutes.

4. Stir in the spinach (which will have collapsed), season to taste and scatter with cashew nuts.

SERVING SUGGESTION
You could serve this with a salad, a bowl of dhal (see page 161), or a dollop of your favourite raita.

SERVES
6

PREP
10 MINS

COOKING
3–5 HRS

SETTING
LOW &
HIGH

Going against all courgette cooking principles, this most unattractive of dishes has beautiful flavours. After all, beauty is more than skin deep – I should know! Serve as a warm vegetable or at room temperature as part of a meze buffet.

Slow-cooked courgettes

4 tbsp extra-virgin olive oil

3 garlic cloves, finely chopped

2–3 dried chillies, crumbled

675g (1½lb) mixed green and yellow courgettes, roughly chopped into 2.5cm (1in) chunks

grated zest of 2 unwaxed or organic lemons and juice of ½ lemon

salt and freshly ground black pepper

2 tbsp roughly chopped flat-leaf parsley

3 tbsp finely chopped mint

1. Heat half the olive oil in a large heavy-based frying pan, add the garlic and chilli and cook over a gentle heat for 2–3 minutes, stirring from time to time; the garlic should be a golden colour. Tip into your slow cooker.

2. Stir in the courgettes and lemon zest and season with salt and pepper. Cover and cook for 3–5 hours on low. The courgettes will gradually collapse, and become very soft.

3. Turn the heat to high and fold in the parsley, mint and lemon juice. Drizzle with the remaining olive oil. Cook, uncovered, for 10 minutes. This dish can be eaten either hot or at room temperature.

Also try
If you grow courgettes, the flowers are delicious to eat; try them battered and deep-fried or stuffed, battered and deep-fried.

SERVES
4–6

PREP
20 MINS

COOKING
6¼–7¼ HRS

SETTING
LOW & HIGH

**If you think you don't like fennel, think again. Here the fennel
loses its aggression, mellows into blissful harmony and then you're
smacked in the mouth with glorious crunchy crumbs.**

Slow-cooked fennel with tomatoes, olives and crispy crumbs

4 fennel bulbs, tough outer layer removed

180ml (6fl oz) extra-virgin olive oil

1 head of garlic, split into cloves and peeled

2 tbsp chopped soft oregano leaves

120ml (4fl oz) dry white wine

400g (14oz) tin good chopped tomatoes

salt and freshly ground black pepper

2 tbsp balsamic vinegar

24 Kalamata olives, stoned and roughly chopped

12 basil leaves, ripped

for the bread topping

2 garlic cloves

1 tbsp soft thyme leaves

2 tsp rosemary leaves

2 tbsp flat-leaf parsley leaves

150ml (¼ pint) good olive oil

2-day-old ciabatta loaf, broken into small pieces

1 tbsp pumpkin seeds

4 tbsp grated Parmesan

to serve

new potatoes or salad

1. Quarter the fennel lengthways, then place in a large frying pan and cook in the olive oil over a medium heat for 15 minutes, turning regularly until golden all over.

2. Add the garlic, oregano, wine, tomatoes and 150ml (¼ pint) boiling water. Bring to the boil and transfer to your slow cooker. Cover and cook on low for 6–7 hours, then season with salt, black pepper and balsamic vinegar. Fold in the olives and basil, then cook, uncovered, on high for 15 minutes.

3. Meanwhile, for the bread topping: finely chop together the garlic and herbs. Heat the olive oil in a frying pan over a medium heat, add the ciabatta pieces and fry until golden. Fold in the remaining ingredients and stir to combine. Scatter over the slow-cooked fennel.

4. Serve this dish either hot or at room temperature with new potatoes or a leafy salad.

SERVES
4

PREP
15 MINS

COOKING
6–8 HRS

SETTING
LOW

A great dip for vegetarians and meat eaters alike. If you thin the
dip with vegetable stock after puréeing, it makes a delicious soup.
And, of course, it's lovely as a vegetable accompaniment.

Red lentil dip

4 tbsp extra-virgin olive oil

4 garlic cloves, finely chopped

1 onion, finely chopped

1 tsp ground cumin

1 tsp ground coriander

1 tsp fennel seeds

½ tsp cayenne pepper

225g (8oz) split red lentils, rinsed
and drained

600ml (1 pint) vegetable stock

2 tbsp sun-dried tomato pesto

1 tbsp lemon juice

salt and freshly ground black pepper

4 spring onions, finely diced

2 tbsp finely chopped flat-leaf parsley

2 tbsp finely chopped coriander

to serve
flat bread or raw vegetable crudités

1. Heat the olive oil in a saucepan, add the garlic and onion and cook over
a medium heat for 8 minutes, until the onion has softened but has not
coloured. Add the spices and cook for a further 2 minutes. Transfer to your
slow cooker.

2. Add the lentils and stock, cover and cook on low for 6–8 hours until the
lentils are tender, adding more hot stock if necessary.

3. Fold in the tomato pesto and lemon juice and beat with a heavy whisk or
wooden spoon until the lentils break up into a thick purée. (I like a textured
finish.) Season to taste and fold in the spring onions, parsley and coriander.

4. Add more olive oil if the purée appears too dry, then serve with flat bread
or raw vegetable crudités.

SERVES 4 · PREP 15 MINS · COOKING 3½–4½ HRS · SETTING LOW & HIGH

At first sight, this seems a strange combination, but think about it and it begins to make sense. The wonderful sweetness of the prunes complements the slightly bitter taste of the aubergine, add in the Asian flavours and you end up with a great vegetarian dish that could be topped with some soured cream and served with a big bowl of spring onion rice.

Spicy braised aubergines with prunes

6 tbsp vegetable oil

1 tbsp sesame oil

2 large shiny aubergines, calyx removed, cut into 2.5cm (1in) cubes

1 tbsp finely chopped garlic

1 tbsp grated fresh ginger

2 bunches spring onions, cut into 2.5cm (1in) batons

400ml (13½fl oz) vegetable stock

2 tbsp soy sauce

175g (6oz) stoned prunes, chopped

1 tbsp salted Chinese black beans, finely chopped (optional)

1 tsp cornflour, mixed to a paste with 2 tbsp water

to garnish

2 tbsp roughly chopped coriander

1 green chilli, deseeded and finely diced

1. In a frying pan, heat the oils and fry the aubergine over a high heat for about 8 minutes, until brown all over. Place in the slow cooker.

2. Add the garlic, ginger and spring onions to the pan and cook for 3 minutes, turning regularly. Combine with the aubergine, add the stock, soy sauce, prunes and black beans, if using, cover and cook on low for 3–4 hours.

3. Increase the heat to high and stir, then add the cornflour paste, cover and cook for 30 minutes to thicken.

4. Spoon the mixture into a dish and scatter with the coriander and chilli. Serve hot or at room temperature.

SERVING SUGGESTION

This is excellent as part of an Asian buffet. I serve it with spring onion rice: fry a few sliced spring onions for a couple of minutes in vegetable oil over a medium heat, then stir in some cooked rice and fry briefly. Season with a splash of Thai fish sauce and garnish with roughly chopped coriander.

SERVES
4

PREP
25 MINS

COOKING
6–8 HRS

SETTING
LOW

A classic recipe, which you don't see very often in cookbooks or for that matter in restaurants. It's delicious and spoon tender, and does wonders for what I believe is essentially a dull vegetable.

Prosciutto-wrapped braised celery

2 heads of celery, trimmed

8 slices of prosciutto (Parma or Serrano ham)

55g (2oz) unsalted butter

1 tbsp olive oil

1 onion, finely chopped

1 carrot, thinly sliced

2 garlic cloves, finely chopped

100g (3½oz) smoked streaky bacon, cut into lardons

½ tsp soft thyme leaves

350g (12oz) piece of pork rind (optional)

1 tsp anchovy essence

60ml (2fl oz) dry red wine

450ml (¾ pint) strong chicken or beef stock

freshly ground black pepper

25g (1oz) Parmesan, grated

1. Cut the leafy tops off each head of celery (retain for another use), leaving a 15cm (6in) heart. Remove strings from the outside stalks. Plunge the celery hearts into boiling salted water and cook for 10 minutes. Drain and set aside to cool slightly, then cut the celery in half lengthways. Wrap each half in 2 slices of prosciutto.

2. Meanwhile, heat the butter and olive oil in a flameproof casserole over a medium heat. Add the onion, carrot, garlic, bacon and thyme and cook for 8 minutes, stirring occasionally.

3. If using, place the pork rind, fat side down, on the bottom of your slow cooker, top with the celery hearts and surround with the vegetables and bacon. Add the anchovy essence, wine and stock. Cover and cook on low for 6–8 hours. Season with pepper to taste.

4. Sprinkle with grated Parmesan and glaze under a hot grill.

SERVING SUGGESTION
You could serve this as a starter or with roast or grilled meat.

Also try
This also works well with 2 heads of fennel.

One of my favourite chutneys and it's perfect for the slow cooker.
It's superb with cold meats and cheese.

Apricot and orange chutney

4 organic oranges, unpeeled, chopped
into 2cm (¾in) pieces and pips
removed

1.5kg (3lb 5oz) apricots, stoned and
quartered

450g (1lb) onions, roughly diced

450g (1lb) caster sugar

1 tsp sea salt

½ tsp cloves

1 tsp freshly ground black pepper

½ tsp dried chilli flakes

½ tsp ground mace

1 tsp medium-hot curry powder

1 tbsp yellow mustard seeds

1 tsp ground turmeric

500ml (18fl oz) cider vinegar

1. Mix together all the ingredients and tip into the slow cooker. Cover and cook on low for 6–7 hours, stirring from time to time, especially near the end of the cooking time.

2. Sterilize 6 clean jam jars by warming them in the bottom of a low oven (120°C/250°F/Gas ½) for 30 minutes. Spoon in the chutney and seal each with a lid.

3. Store for at least a week before consuming. The chutney will keep for up to 6 months in a cool, dry place, but store in the fridge once opened.

SERVING SUGGESTION
This chutney is delicious with red Leicester.

Also try
This can also be made with 750g (1lb 10 oz) dried apricots. Soak them in water for 1 hour, then quarter and cook for the same length of time in the slow cooker.

Roasts & braises

Pot-roast chicken

see page 58

Braised squid with potatoes and peas **54**

Herby salmon fillets **56**

Jerk chicken **57**

Pot-roast chicken **58**

Moroccan spiced roast chicken **60**

Oven-roasted chicken with Med veg **62**

Aromatic chicken with oranges **64**

Spiced garlic and thyme roasted spatchcock chicken **66**

Italian poussin with white beans **68**

Pot-roasted partridge with cider and Calvados **70**

Braised pigeon with pine nuts and raisins **72**

Braised hare with Tolosa beans **74**

Braised sweetbreads with sorrel **75**

Spring lamb with vegetables **76**

Lamb steaks with rosemary garlic flageolet crust **78**

Arabian roast lamb and potatoes **80**

North African mutton with spiced fruits and nuts **82**

Braised calf's liver **83**

Pot-roasted beef with gremolata **84**

Braised beef with baby carrots and horseradish **86**

Pork fillets with prune and parsley stuffing **87**

Garlic and sage pork with fennel and pears **88**

Spicy pork in stout **90**

Poached pork shoulder **92**

Braised gammon and potatoes with a peach and
Barkham Blue cheese sauce **93**

Caramelized pork ribs with bourbon and ginger **94**

SERVES
4

PREP
25 MINS

COOKING
4–6 HRS

SETTING
LOW

This is a cracker! The slow cooker was built with squid in mind: if you're not flash-frying or grilling it, you need a good squidy stew packed with loads of flavour and memories of Mediterranean moments.

Braised squid with potatoes and peas

450g (1lb) potatoes, cut into 2cm (¾in) dice

2 tbsp olive oil

1 onion, finely chopped

800g (1lb 12oz) squid, cleaned and squid tubes thickly sliced

4 garlic cloves, finely chopped

4 tbsp brandy

200ml (6½fl oz) dry white wine

400g (14oz) tin chopped tomatoes

2 tsp tomato purée

1 thyme sprig

1 bay leaf

1 tsp smoked paprika

salt and freshly ground black pepper

150g (5½oz) shelled fresh peas, or frozen peas, defrosted

to garnish

roughly chopped flat-leaf parsley (optional)

to serve

torn chunks of crusty country bread

1. Add the potatoes to a saucepan of boiling water and parboil for 2–3 minutes. Drain.

2. Heat the oil in a large frying pan, add the onion and fry over a medium heat, until just beginning to turn golden. Stir in the squid and garlic and cook for 2–3 minutes.

3. Warm the brandy in a small saucepan, flame with a match, then carefully pour into the squid. When the flames subside, add the wine, tomatoes, tomato purée, herbs, paprika and seasoning.

4. Bring to the boil, then tip into the slow cooker pot. Cover and cook on low for 4–6 hours, until the squid is tender.

5. Cook the peas in a pan of boiling water for 3 minutes just before you are ready to serve. Drain and stir into the squid.

6. Serve in shallow bowls sprinkled with a little chopped parsley, if you like, and torn bread to mop up the juices.

TO MAKE IT SPICIER
For chilli fans, add 2 deseeded and finely chopped green chillies as well as the paprika.

Also try
You could also throw in some mussels and clams. Clean and discard any that do not close when tapped against the sink. For the last hour of cooking the braised squid, turn the slow cooker to high, add the shellfish, then cover and cook. Before serving, discard any mussels or clams that have not opened.

Salmon is great fish for withstanding and accepting big flavours, and there are plenty of them in this dish. Keep the accompaniments simple: just a leafy salad and a few new potatoes.

Herby salmon fillets

4 x 175g (6oz) salmon fillets, skin on

300ml (½ pint) fish or vegetable stock, hot

for the marinade

4 long mild green chillies, roughly chopped

4 garlic cloves, roughly chopped

1 bunch coriander, roughly chopped

1 bunch basil, roughly chopped

8 mint leaves

2cm (3/4in) piece of fresh ginger, roughly chopped

juice and grated zest of 2 unwaxed or organic lemons

4 tbsp rapeseed or vegetable oil

to serve

fresh salad

boiled potatoes

1. For the marinade, blend the chillies, garlic, half the coriander, half the basil, the mint, ginger, lemon juice and zest and oil in a blender or food processor until smooth.

2. Pour the marinade over the salmon and massage well to combine. Leave, covered, at room temperature for 30 minutes.

3. After 30 minutes place the salmon fillets with the marinade and stock in your slow cooker and cook on low for 3–4 hours.

4. At the end of the cooking time, fold the remaining coriander and basil into the salmon. This will enhance the green of the dish, as by the time it has finished cooking the herb paste will have turned to dull olive green; the addition of these herbs will revitalize the colour.

5. Serve the salmon fillets with a simple salad and boiled potatoes.

SERVES 4   PREP 30 MINS   MARINATE 1 HR   COOKING 6–8 HRS   SETTING LOW

I recently took part in a "jerk" (hot spice-rubbed meat) challenge on the beautiful island of Jamaica. I didn't win, but I did learn a thing or two, so I reckon my version is pretty authentic apart from the honey. I love the little bit of sweetness it adds, which contrasts perfectly with the fire of the chillies.

Jerk chicken

2 tbsp vegetable oil

12 chicken thigh fillets, skin and flesh slashed 3 times on each

2 onions, finely chopped

1 tbsp plain flour

3 Scotch bonnet chillies

1 tbsp tomato purée

300ml (½ pint) chicken stock

for the marinade

3 mild red chillies, roughly chopped

2 bunches spring onions, roughly chopped

2 garlic cloves, roughly chopped

¼ tsp grated nutmeg

2.5cm (1in) piece of fresh ginger, roughly chopped

½ tsp ground cinnamon

½ bunch thyme, roughly chopped

1 tbsp vegetable oil

1 tbsp runny honey

1 tbsp lime juice

1 tsp salt

freshly ground black pepper

to serve

home-made coleslaw, (see page 94)

long-grain rice

1. Put half the oil in a frying pan over a high heat and brown the chicken pieces all over. Set aside to cool.

2. Use a food processor or a mortar and pestle to make the marinade. Blitz or crush all the ingredients into a smooth paste. Transfer to a bowl.

3. Toss the browned chicken pieces in the marinade, cover with cling film and refrigerate for at least 1 hour, but preferably overnight.

4. Heat the remaining oil in a frying pan and cook the onions over a medium heat for 8–10 minutes, until softened and pale golden. Transfer to the slow cooker and sprinkle with the flour, stir to combine, then add the Scotch bonnet chillies and tomato purée. Stir once again and add the stock, chicken and marinade.

5. Cover and cook on low for 6–8 hours (halfway through, check the taste of the sauce: once it is hot enough remove the Scotch bonnet chillies and discard), until the chicken is thoroughly cooked.

6. Serve with home-made apple coleslaw (see page 94) and rice.

SERVES
4

PREP
20 MINS

COOKING
7¼–8¼
HRS

SETTING
LOW &
HIGH

An all-time family favourite, which features at least once a month on my household's domestic menu. Get the main structure of the pot-roast right and your choice of vegetables can vary with the season.

Pot-roast chicken

1–2 tbsp olive oil

1.5kg (3lb 5oz) free-range chicken

115g (4oz) smoked streaky bacon, chopped

1 onion, roughly chopped

3 garlic cloves, finely chopped

2 celery sticks, cut into 2.5cm (1in) chunks

2 carrots, cut into 2.5cm (1in) chunks

12 baby new potatoes

1 tbsp soft thyme leaves

2 bay leaves

400g (14oz) tin chopped tomatoes

1 tbsp Worcestershire sauce

850ml (1½ pints) chicken or vegetable stock, hot

225g (8oz) broccoli florets

115g (4oz) frozen peas, defrosted

handful of spinach

115g (4oz) frozen baby broad beans, defrosted

salt and freshly ground black pepper

1. Place a large frying pan over a high heat, add the olive oil and, when hot, add the whole chicken to the pan, turning occasionally until brown all over. Remove and place in your slow cooker.

2. Add the bacon to the frying pan and fry for a few minutes over a medium heat, then add the onion, garlic, celery, carrots, potatoes, thyme and bay leaves and cook for a further 6 minutes.

3. Add the tomatoes and the Worcestershire sauce and bring to the boil. Spoon into your slow cooker, add the stock, then cover and cook on low for 7–8 hours until the chicken is cooked. To check if the chicken is cooked through, push a skewer right into the thickest part of the thigh; if the juices run clear it is cooked – any pink and it needs a bit longer.

4. Lift out the chicken onto a platter, cover with foil and set aside in a warm place to rest. Turn the slow cooker to high, stir the green vegetables into the pot and cook, uncovered, for 10 minutes until the vegetables are tender. Season to taste.

5. Carve the chicken. Spoon the vegetables and broth into 4 warm bowls.

Also try
Use chicken thighs (bone in) instead of a whole chicken for a quicker supper: reduce the cooking time on low by half to 3½–4 hours.

SERVES
4

PREP
15 MINS

MARINATE
3½ HRS

COOKING
2 HRS

OVEN

If you're looking to add a little flavour to a rather bland chicken, this is the perfect recipe. I haven't found a better way of livening up the Sunday roast.

Moroccan spiced roast chicken

1.5kg (3lb 5oz) chicken

for the rub

1 bulb of garlic

2 tbsp olive oil

2 tbsp caraway seeds

1 tbsp cumin seeds

2 tsp ground turmeric

3 tsp dried rosemary

1½ tsp dried oregano

4 tbsp sea salt

½ bunch coriander, roughly chopped

6 tbsp harissa paste

2 tsp caster sugar

1 small onion, roughly chopped

2 tbsp Greek yoghurt

freshly ground black pepper

to serve

couscous

leafy salad

1. Preheat the oven to 180°C/350°F/Gas 4. Cut 1cm (½in) off the top of the garlic bulb, drizzle a little of the oil over the cut surface, wrap in foil and cook in the oven for 30 minutes. Allow to cool enough to handle, then unwrap, separate the garlic cloves and squeeze the flesh from their papery wrapping. Turn the oven off and set aside.

2. Grind all the dried spices, dried herbs and salt in a pestle and mortar (or electric coffee grinder), then combine with the garlic and all the other ingredients for the rub, including the remaining oil, in a food processor and purée until smooth. (This will keep in the fridge for up to 2 weeks.)

3. Rub 2 tbsp of the rub over the skin and the cavity of the chicken, cover with cling film and refrigerate for at least 3 hours, but preferably overnight. Take the chicken out of the fridge and allow it to come to room temperature for at least 30 minutes.

4. Preheat the oven to 180°C/350°F/Gas 4.

5. Roast the chicken for 1½ hours until the meat is cooked and the juices run clear when the thickest part of the thigh is pierced with a skewer, then allow to rest for 10 minutes before carving.

6. Serve with couscous and a leafy salad.

There's something special to be said for a dish that comes fully loaded so that you've no need for lots of pans and the washing-up is greatly reduced. I've suggested some vegetables, but please feel free to mix and match.

Oven-roasted chicken with Med veg

1.5kg (3lb 5oz) free-range chicken

150ml (¼ pint) good olive oil

salt and freshly ground black pepper

½ lemon

½ white onion, peeled

4 thyme sprigs

2 bay leaves

325g (11½oz) Ratte, Anya or Pink Fir Apple new potatoes

1 small aubergine, calyx removed, cut into 2.5cm (1in) dice

½ butternut squash, peeled, deseeded and cut into 2.5cm (1in) dice

1 red onion, cut into quarters

1 fennel bulb, tough outer layer removed, quartered lengthways

2 courgettes, cut into 2.5cm (1in) discs

12 garlic cloves, unpeeled

3 tbsp good balsamic vinegar

1 tbsp marjoram or oregano leaves

1. Preheat the oven to 200°C/400°F/Gas 6.

2. Rub the chicken all over with 2 tbsp olive oil and season with salt and pepper. Place the lemon, white onion, 1 thyme sprig and the bay leaves inside the cavity of the chicken.

3. Place the chicken on a roasting tray with the new potatoes and roast for 30 minutes. Add the aubergine, squash, red onion and fennel and douse with the remaining olive oil, return to the oven and cook for a further 30 minutes before adding the courgettes, garlic and the remaining thyme. Toss with the other vegetables, season and return to the oven for 30 minutes, basting and turning the vegetables regularly, until the chicken is cooked through and the juices run clear when the thickest part of the thigh is pierced with a skewer.

4. Remove the chicken to a warm platter, cover loosely with foil and keep warm while it rests.

5. Meanwhile, place the roasting tray with the vegetables on your hob over a medium heat, add the balsamic vinegar and marjoram and toss together with the roasting juices. Spoon the vegetables and juices around the chicken.

SERVES
4

PREP
15 MINS

COOKING
6½–8½
HRS

SETTING
LOW &
HIGH

A beautifully flavoured chicken dish inspired by the rustic cuisine of Spain. You can also fold in some blanched broad beans and peas, if the mood grabs you, for the last 10 minutes of cooking.

Aromatic chicken with oranges

4 tbsp olive oil

4 chicken breasts, skin on

4 chicken thigh fillets, skin on

4 cloves

3 organic oranges, unpeeled and cut into 2.5cm (1in) chunks

4 garlic cloves, crushed to a paste with a little sea salt

85g (3oz) pancetta, diced or lardons

4 thyme sprigs

450g (1lb) pickling onions or small shallots, peeled

1 unwaxed or organic lemon, cut into 2.5cm (1in) chunks

1 tsp smoked paprika

180ml (6fl oz) Manzanilla sherry

salt and freshly ground black pepper

to garnish

40g (1½oz) flaked almonds, toasted

to serve

toasted chunks of country bread

garlic clove

new potatoes

1. Put the oil in a large frying pan over a medium heat, then fry the chicken breasts and thighs until brown all over. Transfer the chicken with tongs or a slotted spoon to your slow cooker.

2. Poke the cloves into the orange pieces.

3. Add the garlic, pancetta, thyme, onions, clove-studded orange pieces and lemon to the frying pan and fry for 5 minutes, until the onions are brown. Stir in the paprika.

4. Place this mixture in your slow cooker on top of the chicken. Add the sherry and 290ml (9½fl oz) water, cover and cook on low for 6–8 hours, until the chicken is thoroughly cooked.

5. Remove the chicken pieces with half the fruit and onions, and keep them warm.

6. Turn the slow cooker to high, and cook the remaining fruit and onions, uncovered, for 20 minutes, then mash the sauce, roughly crushing the fruit and onions.

7. Return the chicken with the reserved fruit and onions to the slow cooker pot, season to taste, then cover and warm through on high for 10 minutes.

8. Spoon the sauce over the chicken and scatter over a few toasted flaked almonds. Serve with a toasted chunk of country bread rubbed with a garlic clove and new potatoes.

Also try
Try cooking this with rabbit pieces instead of chicken breasts and thighs. Use a similar quantity of meat and the same cooking times.

SERVES
4

PREP
20 MINS

COOKING
6 HRS

SETTING
LOW

Spatchcocking is when you (or your butcher) split the chicken down the length of its backbone and spread the bird out flat. This recipe has a lovely balance of sweet and sour from the sugar and lemon.

Spiced garlic and thyme roasted spatchcock chicken

60ml (2fl oz) extra-virgin olive oil

1.5 kg (3lb 5oz) free-range chicken, spatchcocked

1 tsp dried chilli flakes

3 garlic cloves, crushed to a paste with a little sea salt

½ tsp smoked paprika

3 tsp dried thyme

grated zest and juice of 1 unwaxed or organic lemon

60ml (2fl oz) sherry vinegar

2 tbsp dark muscovado sugar

½ tsp freshly ground black pepper

4 thyme sprigs

1 unwaxed or organic lemon, halved

1. Heat a little of the olive oil in a large non-stick frying pan and brown the chicken on both sides over a high heat, until golden. Place the chicken in the slow cooker. Mix all the remaining ingredients together, add to the chicken and stir to combine.

2. Cover with the lid and cook on low for 6 hours or until the chicken is thoroughly cooked and the juices run clear when pierced with a skewer.

3. Lift out the chicken onto a warmed serving platter, cover with foil and allow to rest for 15 minutes. Drizzle with any cooking juices and serve.

SERVING SUGGESTION
This is lovely in the summer with a salad or in the winter with roasted vegetables and mashed potato.

How to spatchcock a chicken
To spatchcock: split the chicken lengthways down the length of the backbone with a knife or poultry shears and remove the backbone and small rib bones, then turn the bird over and press down to flatten it. Or ask your butcher to do this for you.

SERVES
4

PREP
20 MINS

SOAK
1 HR

COOKING
6½ HRS

SETTING
LOW &
HIGH

An Italian-influenced dish that makes good use of a good-value bird. It works just as well with chicken breast, but you lose the wow factor.

Italian poussin with white beans

2 tbsp raisins

7 tbsp sweet wine, eg *vin santo*

2 large free-range poussin, split in half

2 tbsp red wine vinegar

4 tbsp olive oil

4 Italian sausages or your favourite meaty sausages, ideally flavoured with fennel

1 onion, finely chopped

1 tsp soft thyme leaves

1 celery stick, finely diced

1 garlic clove, crushed to a paste with a little sea salt

1 bay leaf

200g (7oz) tin chopped tomatoes

2 tbsp caster sugar

400g (14oz) tin cannellini or haricot beans, drained and rinsed

2 tbsp pine nuts, toasted

1. Place the raisins in a bowl with 3 tbsp sweet wine, cover and leave to soak for at least 1 hour but preferably overnight.

2. Snip out the ribcage in the poussin halves, leaving the breast attached to the leg and thigh.

3. Place the poussin in a bowl and pour over the wine vinegar, 3 tbsp olive oil and the remaining sweet wine. Cover and set aside to marinate for 15 minutes, then drain, reserving the marinade.

4. Warm 1 tbsp olive oil in a frying pan over a high heat, then brown the sausages and poussin. Remove and set aside. Add the onion, thyme, celery, garlic and bay leaf and pan-fry over a low heat for 6–8 minutes, stirring from time to time. Spoon into the slow cooker. Add the marinade, tomatoes and sugar with a little water (about 75ml/2½fl oz), then cover and cook on low for 6 hours until the meat is cooked through.

5. Lift out the poussin and sausages onto a warm platter. Cover and keep warm. Add the beans, raisins with their soaking liquid and pine nuts to the cooking juices in the slow cooker. Turn to high, cover with a lid and cook for 20 minutes. Return the poussin and sausages to the sauce, cover and heat through for a further 10 minutes.

SERVING SUGGESTION
This is a one-pot supper, but a salad or green vegetable is good with it too.

Why oh why don't we eat more game? It's good value, nutritious, very low in saturated fat and by the by it tastes fabulous. This recipe could also be used for pheasant, in which case double the cooking time on low and use two birds instead of four.

Pot-roasted partridge with cider and Calvados

55g (2oz) butter

4 partridge

salt and freshly ground black pepper

1 medium onion, diced

85g (3oz) bacon lardons

1 celery stick, coarsely chopped

1 carrot, coarsely chopped

4 sage sprigs

1 Granny Smith apple, peeled, cored and cut into large chunks

1 Bramley apple, peeled, cored and cut into large chunks

60ml (2fl oz) Calvados, plus 2 tbsp

300ml (½ pint) dry cider

150ml (¼ pint) double cream

4 tbsp finely chopped flat-leaf parsley

1 tsp finely chopped tarragon

to serve

buttered cabbage

new potatoes

1. Melt the butter in a large frying pan. Season the partridge and fry over a medium heat until pale golden all over. Remove with tongs and place in your slow cooker.

2. Add the onion, lardons, celery, carrot and sage sprigs to the frying pan and cook over a medium heat for about 8 minutes, until the onion is soft and translucent and the lardons are crispy. Carefully pour off any excess fat that has emerged from the lardons, then add the vegetable mixture to the slow cooker.

3. Sprinkle over the apple chunks, then pour over 60ml (2fl oz) Calvados. Set the Calvados alight, then once the flames have died down, add the cider. Cover the cooker with the lid and cook on low for 4–6 hours until the meat is cooked.

4. Push the sauce through a fine-meshed sieve into a bowl. Pour this strained sauce back into the slow cooker, add 2 tbsp Calvados, increase the heat to high and cook, uncovered, for 20 minutes. Add the cream and whisk together. Cover and cook for a further 10 minutes until the sauce is creamy and slightly thickened. Fold in the parsley and tarragon and season to taste.

5. Spoon the sauce over the partridge and serve with buttered cabbage and new potatoes.

SERVING SUGGESTION
Peel and core 450g (1lb) Cox's apples and cut into 8 segments. Pan-fry in 25g (1oz) unsalted butter with 55g (2oz) soft dark brown sugar over a medium heat for about 8 minutes, turning from time to time, until golden. Serve immediately with the partridge.

The humble woodpigeon deserves a little love and effort to extract its best qualities. It represents great value, but of course, you could always buy expensive corn-fed pigeon (squab) if you want more of a dinner-party dish.

Braised pigeon with pine nuts and raisins

4 woodpigeons, cleaned

4 tbsp red wine vinegar

6 tbsp olive oil

150ml (¼ pint) *vin santo* or other sweet wine

115g (4oz) smoked streaky bacon, diced or pancetta pieces

1 onion, finely chopped

1 carrot, diced

2 celery sticks, diced

2 garlic cloves, crushed

1 bay leaf

4 tbsp raisins

2 tbsp pine nuts, toasted

to serve

green vegetables

mashed potato

1. Split the pigeons in half, cutting through and removing the breastbone, so that you have 8 pieces. Place the pigeons in a non-metallic bowl. Pour over the wine vinegar, 3 tbsp olive oil and 2 tbsp of the *vin santo*. Cover and set aside to marinate for at least 1 hour at room temperature, or overnight in the fridge. Drain.

2. Warm 3 tbsp olive oil in a frying pan. Add the bacon, onion, carrot, celery, garlic and bay leaf and pan-fry over a low heat for 8–10 minutes until the vegetables are starting to colour. Stir to combine.

3. Lay the pigeon halves in the slow cooker, add the vegetable mix and the remaining *vin santo* plus the marinade and 75ml (2½fl oz) water, then cover and cook on low for 2½–3 hours until the meat is cooked through.

4. Meanwhile, soak the raisins in warm water for 20 minutes, then drain.

5. Lift the pigeon halves onto a warm platter. Add the raisins and pine nuts to the pan juices and vegetables, then spoon over the pigeon.

6. Serve with green vegetables and mash.

SERVES
4

PREP
25 MINS

MARINATE
8 HRS

COOKING
6¾–7¾
HRS

SETTING
LOW &
HIGH

Hare is fast disappearing from the UK's culinary repertoire, which is a shame as I think it's one of our best game meats. This is a delicious one-pot dish inspired by the Spanish Tolosa bean (Basque black bean) stews.

Braised hare with Tolosa beans

8 hare pieces, preferably haunch legs
salt and freshly ground black pepper

for the marinade
1 tsp finely chopped soft thyme leaves
1 bay leaf
1 onion, finely sliced
1 garlic clove, finely chopped
2 tbsp Armagnac

for the beans
1 onion, finely chopped
2 garlic cloves, finely chopped
120ml (4fl oz) extra-virgin olive oil
pinch of cayenne pepper
225g (8oz) chorizo sausage, sliced into
   2.5cm (1in) chunks
225g (8oz) blood sausage or good black
   pudding, cut into 2.5cm (1in) chunks
400g (14oz) tin red kidney beans,
   rinsed and drained
100g (3½oz) smoked streaky bacon,
   diced
600ml (1 pint) chicken stock or water
675g (1½lb) Savoy cabbage, shredded

to serve
creamy mashed potato
gremolata (see page 84)

1. Wash the hare pieces, place them in a bowl and mix with all the marinade ingredients, then season to taste. Cover with cling film, refrigerate and marinate for at least 8 hours, turning from time to time.

2. For the beans, gently fry the onion and the garlic in half the oil with the cayenne for about 8 minutes, until the onion has softened but not browned.

3. Increase the heat, add the chorizo and blood sausage and cook for 5 minutes to release the fat.

4. Add the hare pieces to the pan and brown all over. Spoon into your slow cooker, then stir in the beans, bacon, sausage mix and stock, cover and cook on low for 6–7 hours.

5. Turn the slow cooker to high, then add the cabbage and cook for a further 40 minutes.

6. Spoon the beans and meat into 4 warm bowls and serve with creamy mash and a sprinkling of gremolata (see page 84).

SERVES
4

PREP
20 MINS

SOAK
12 HRS

COOKING
5¼–6¼
HRS

SETTING
LOW &
HIGH

A classic French combination, the sorrel adds citrusy notes, which help to cut the richness of the sweetbreads. If you can order the sweetbreads through a decent butcher you'll find this dish easy and delicious.

Braised sweetbreads with sorrel

4 calf's sweetbreads, soaked for
    12 hours in several changes of
    cold water
3 carrots, thinly sliced
2 celery sticks, thinly sliced
16 baby onions, peeled
55g (2oz) unsalted butter
2 garlic cloves, finely chopped
1 tsp soft thyme leaves
400g (14oz) tin chopped tomatoes
120ml (4fl oz) dry white wine
120ml (4fl oz) chicken stock
175g (6oz) frozen petits pois, defrosted
225g (8oz) peeled raw tiger prawns
3 handfuls sorrel
150ml (¼ pint) double cream
salt and freshly ground black pepper

to serve
mashed potato

1. Blanch the sweetbreads in boiling salted water for 5 minutes, plunge into cold water, then remove all the sinews and transparent skin and leave whole.

2. In a frying pan, gently cook the carrots, celery and onions in half the butter for 10 minutes. Add the garlic, thyme and sweetbreads and fry until the sweetbreads are lightly coloured. Transfer the mix to your slow cooker and add the tomatoes, white wine and stock, then cover and cook on a low setting for 5–6 hours until the sweetbreads are cooked.

3. Turn the slow cooker to high, add the peas and prawns, cover and cook for 15 minutes. Remove the sweetbreads, prawns and vegetables and keep warm.

4. Meanwhile, place the remaining butter in a saucepan over a low heat. Add the sorrel and cook, stirring occasionally, until it has broken down.

5. Strain the cooking juices from the slow cooker onto the sorrel and boil until the sauce has reduced by half. Stir in the cream and season to taste. Return the solids to the sauce and cook, uncovered, for a further 15 minutes.

6. Slice the sweetbreads and arrange on 4 warm plates with the prawns and vegetables. Spoon over the prawns and vegetables with the sauce and serve with mashed potato.

Also try
If you can't find sorrel, try using spinach with lemon juice: the spinach won't break down like the sorrel in step 4 so will need liquidizing.

SERVES 4 · PREP 20 MINS · COOKING 8–10 HRS · SETTING LOW

The arrival of new-season lamb heralds the start of the British growing season – longer evenings, the sun with warmth, time to garden – and so here I bring the two together using a good-value cut and some lovely baby veg.

Spring lamb with vegetables

2 tbsp olive oil

8 lamb shoulder steaks (about 675g/1½lb)

4 cloves

12 baby shallots, peeled (about 250g/9oz)

2 small leeks, thickly sliced, white and green parts kept separate

1 fennel bulb, tough outer layer removed, halved and sliced

2 tbsp plain flour

200ml (6½fl oz) red wine

600ml (1 pint) lamb stock

8 juniper berries

salt and freshly ground black pepper

400g (14oz) baby new potatoes

1 head of garlic, cut in half horizontally

1 bouquet garni

225g (8oz) baby Chantenay carrots, trimmed and scrubbed

8 baby turnips, tops trimmed to about 1cm (½in)

½ small Savoy cabbage, cut into quarters

to serve

salsa verde (optional)

1. Heat the oil in a large frying pan, add the lamb and brown on both sides over a high heat for about 6 minutes. Lift out and put on a plate.

2. Press the cloves into 4 shallots, then add all the shallots, the white sliced leeks (reserve the green slices for later) and fennel to the frying pan. Cook for 3–4 minutes over a medium heat until just beginning to brown, then sprinkle over the flour and mix together. Cook for a further 2–3 minutes, stirring regularly. Stir in the red wine, stock, juniper berries and plenty of seasoning and bring to the boil.

3. Put the potatoes in the base of the slow cooker, arrange the lamb steaks on top, then tuck in the halved garlic bulb and bouquet garni. Pour over the vegetable and hot wine mixture. Cover and cook on low for 8–10 hours, until the lamb is cooked and the potatoes are tender.

4. When you are almost ready to serve, boil the carrots and turnips for 8–10 minutes; steam the cabbage for 8–10 minutes and the green leek tops (but don't mix with the cabbage) for the last 3 minutes, until all the vegetables are just tender.

5. Drain the vegetables and stir the carrots, turnips and leeks into the lamb. Ladle into shallow soup bowls and serve the cabbage to one side. For extra punch, serve the lamb topped with spoonfuls of salsa verde (see below).

FOR THE SALSA VERDE
In a food processor, blitz 3 garlic cloves, 3 sliced spring onions, 2 finely chopped green chillies, 3 chopped anchovy fillets in oil (drained), 3 tbsp capers (rinsed) and a small bunch each of coriander and parsley, until finely chopped. Add 1½ tbsp lemon juice, 1½ tbsp red wine and 40g (1½oz) fresh white breadcrumbs. Slowly mix in up to 210ml (7fl oz) olive oil to make a coarse pesto-like sauce. Season to taste and chill.

Antony's tips
Neck of lamb pieces can be used instead of shoulder steaks. They taste delicious and are a great budget cut (many people are put off by the bones).

A classic partnership of lamb with rosemary and a complete dish with no other additions necessary. If flageolet beans are not available, feel free to use white cannellini or haricot beans.

Lamb steaks with rosemary garlic flageolet crust

2 tbsp good olive oil

4 smoked streaky bacon rashers, cut into lardons

4 garlic cloves, finely chopped

3 anchovies in oil, drained and roughly chopped

2 onions, roughly chopped

1 carrot, roughly chopped

1 celery stick, finely chopped

1 tbsp rosemary leaves, very finely chopped

2 x 400g (14oz) tins flageolet beans, drained and rinsed

salt and freshly ground black pepper

55g (2oz) unsalted butter

4 lamb leg steaks or chump chops

150ml (¼ pint) red wine

150ml (¼ pint) lamb stock

4 tbsp fresh white breadcrumbs

40g (1½oz) Parmesan, grated

1. In a frying pan, heat half the olive oil, add the bacon and cook for 5 minutes over a medium heat. Add the garlic, anchovies, onions, carrot, celery and rosemary and gently cook for 8 minutes, stirring occasionally, until the onion has softened. Add the beans and stir to combine. Season and set aside.

2. In the same frying pan, heat the remaining olive oil and butter and cook the lamb steaks over a high heat for 3 minutes on each side, until they are lightly browned.

3. Spoon a layer of the bean mix into your slow cooker, place the lamb steaks on top, then add the remaining beans. Pour in the wine and stock, cover and cook on low for 6 hours until the meat is cooked.

4. Mix together the breadcrumbs and Parmesan and scatter over the beans. Place the slow cooker pot under a hot grill to brown.

SERVES
6–8

PREP
20 MINS

MARINATE
2 HRS

COOKING
2½ HRS

OVEN

This is roast lamb with attitude. Loads of garlic, hints of chilli and
the aroma of lemon all go towards making your Sunday roast just a
little bit different.

Arabian roast lamb and potatoes

1 leg of lamb

6 garlic cloves, halved

2 tbsp rose harissa paste

juice and grated zest of 1 unwaxed or
organic lemon

pinch of saffron strands, soaked in
1 tbsp very hot water

1 tsp mint leaves

1 tbsp coriander leaves

4 tbsp olive oil

450g (1lb) floury potatoes, cut into
1cm (½in) slices

2 large onions, thickly sliced

salt and freshly ground black pepper

to serve

couscous

spinach

natural yoghurt

1. Make a dozen incisions in the lamb about 2cm (¾in) deep and long.

2. In a mini food processor or mortar and pestle, blend the garlic, harissa, lemon juice and zest, saffron and water, mint, coriander and half the oil to a rough paste. Spread three-quarters of this paste over the lamb, pushing it into the cuts. Place the lamb in a large bowl and cover with cling film. Refrigerate and leave to marinate for at least 2 hours, but ideally overnight.

3. Preheat the oven to 180°C/350°F/Gas 4.

4. Mix the potatoes, onions and the remaining oil and spice paste together and tip into a roasting tin, then place the lamb on top. Season well and roast in the oven for 2 hours until the meat is cooked, basting from time to time and turning the potatoes and onions.

5. Remove from the oven and lift out the lamb onto a platter. Cover with foil and rest in a warm place for 15–20 minutes.

6. Increase the oven temperature to 200°C/400°F/Gas 6 and return the roasting tin to the oven for about 20 minutes more to brown the potatoes.

7. Serve with couscous and spinach, and drizzle with yoghurt.

I use mutton here because I love it, and it's perfect for slow cooking with a really bold flavour. You may have trouble sourcing mutton, so unless you know a good butcher, feel free to use a shoulder of lamb instead.

North African mutton with spiced fruits and nuts

85g (3oz) prunes, stoned and halved

85g (3oz) dried apricots, quartered

300ml (½ pint) strong black tea, hot

2 tbsp argan oil or vegetable oil

1kg (2lb 4oz) shoulder of mutton, most of the fat removed, cut into 5cm (2in) chunks

2 onions, finely chopped

½ tsp ground turmeric

½ tsp ground ginger

¼ tsp grated nutmeg

1½ tsp ground cinnamon

pinch of saffron strands

2 tsp harissa paste

2 tbsp runny honey

200ml (6½fl oz) hot lamb or beef stock

4 tbsp Greek yoghurt

1 tbsp finely chopped mint

55g (2oz) flaked almonds, toasted

3 tbsp roughly chopped coriander

1. Soak the prunes and apricots in the tea for 30 minutes, stirring from time to time.

2. Put half the oil in a frying pan over a high heat, add the mutton and brown all over. Remove and set aside.

3. Add the remaining oil to the frying pan and fry the onions over a medium heat for about 8 minutes, until soft and lightly golden. Add the spices, stir to combine and cook for 1 minute. Spoon this mixture into your slow cooker and top with the mutton and soaked fruits and their liquor.

4. Stir in two-thirds of the harissa, two-thirds of the honey and all the stock, cover and cook on high for 1½ hours, then turn the slow cooker to low, cover again and cook for a further 8 hours, until the meat is cooked.

5. Meanwhile, combine the remaining harissa and honey with the yoghurt and mint and refrigerate until needed.

6. Sprinkle the stew with the almonds and coriander, and serve with the yoghurt on the side.

Aragan oil
Argan oil has a unique, nutty taste. Most of it comes from southern Morocco, where Berber women constantly race the local goats – which have a remarkable ability to climb trees – to collect the prized nuts of the argan tree.

SERVES
4–6

PREP
20 MINS

COOKING
6½–8½
HRS

SETTING
LOW &
HIGH

This is quite a cheffy dish, but then I am a chef and you would expect me to run to a couple of quirky dishes. If you love liver, you'll go for this one. If you prefer lamb's liver, reduce the cooking time on low to 4–6 hours.

Braised calf's liver

1 tbsp olive oil

25g (1oz) butter

1kg (2lb 4oz) piece of calf's liver, cut from the thickest section

salt and freshly ground black pepper

175g (6oz) smoked streaky bacon, cut into lardons

175g (6oz) onion, roughly chopped

225g (8oz) carrot, roughly sliced

1 leek, thinly sliced

4 garlic cloves, roughly chopped

200g (7oz) tin chopped tomatoes

2 bay leaves

2 thyme sprigs

1 celery stick, thinly sliced

½ bottle red wine

1 tsp caster sugar

1 tbsp Worcestershire sauce

2 tbsp brandy (optional)

2 tbsp finely chopped flat-leaf parsley

to serve

buttered peas

mashed potato

1. Put the oil and butter in a frying pan over a high heat and brown the liver all over. Season and set aside.

2. Add the bacon to the frying pan and cook over a medium heat for 8–10 minutes, until golden, then remove half and set aside.

3. Add the onion, carrot, leek and garlic to the bacon in the pan and cook for a further 6–8 minutes to soften and colour the vegetables. Spoon into your slow cooker. Add the liver, tomatoes, herbs, celery, wine, sugar and Worcestershire sauce. Stir to combine, then cover and cook on low for 6–8 hours, until the liver is cooked.

4. Remove the liver, cover with foil and keep warm. There should be plenty of juices in the slow cooker pot. Liquidize the juices with the vegetables and bacon, then pass though a fine sieve and return to the slow cooker with the liver and reserved bacon. Cover and cook on high for 20 minutes. Add the brandy, if using, and parsley and stir to combine.

5. Carve the liver into slices, whatever thickness you like, spoon over the sauce and serve with buttered peas and mash.

SERVES
4

PREP
30 MINS

COOKING
8¼ HRS

SETTING
LOW &
HIGH

Even before I discovered the merits of the slow cooker, I loved pot-roasts, as they're perfect for one-pot dining. If gremolata is not for you, serve this with a dollop of pesto mixed with soured cream.

Pot-roasted beef with gremolata

60ml (2fl oz) olive oil

4 small floury potatoes, unpeeled, washed and halved

2 parsnips, peeled and roughly chopped in 2cm (¾in) pieces

350g (12oz) butternut squash, unpeeled, deseeded and cut into 4 wedges

350g (12oz) baby Chantenay carrots, trimmed and scrubbed

12 baby onions, peeled whole, leaving as much of the root on as possible

850g (1lb 14oz) piece of beef rump, topside or brisket

2 tbsp wholegrain mustard

6 garlic cloves, peeled

12 thyme sprigs

1 tbsp smoked paprika

sea salt and freshly ground black pepper

1 tbsp Worcestershire sauce

1 tbsp tomato purée

375ml (12½fl oz) beef stock

120ml (4fl oz) red wine

15g (½oz) gravy thickener

for the gremolata

2 tbsp finely chopped flat-leaf parsley

1 garlic clove, finely chopped

grated zest of 1 unwaxed or organic lemon

1. Heat the oil in a frying pan and cook in batches over a medium heat the potatoes, parsnips, butternut squash, carrots and onions, until golden brown. Spoon this mixture into the bottom of your slow cooker.

2. In the same pan with the residual oil, fry the beef until brown all over.

3. Meanwhile, in a mini food processor, blend together the mustard, garlic, thyme and paprika with a little sea salt until smooth, then stir in the Worcestershire sauce and tomato purée.

4. Spread this mixture over the beef, then place the joint on top of the vegetables. Add the beef stock and wine, cover and cook on low for 8 hours until the meat is cooked through.

5. Remove the beef, cover loosely with foil and set aside to rest.

6. Turn the cooker to high. Whisk the gravy thickener with 2 tbsp water and stir it into the liquid and vegetables in the cooker. Cover and cook for 15 minutes until lightly thickened. Check the seasoning.

7. Slice the beef and arrange on 4 warm plates, then top with the vegetables and sauce. Combine the ingredients for the gremolata and sprinkle over each portion.

Gravy tip
After thickening the sauce, add 1 tbsp verjuice or balsamic vinegar for a taste explosion.

SERVES 4 | PREP 20 MINS | COOKING 8½–10½ HRS | SETTING LOW & HIGH

Using the cheaper cuts of meat is a dying skill, but if we don't buy the animal's forequarters it means the price of its hindquarters – the luxury end – keeps going up. Plus there is always the bonus of a magical flavour. Braising steak, which is used here, is a perfect cut for your slow cooker.

Braised beef with baby carrots and horseradish

4 x 225g (8oz) braising steaks

55g (2oz) seasoned plain flour

2 tbsp dripping, lard or vegetable oil

2 onions, roughly chopped

1 celery stick, finely sliced

1 thyme sprig

2 bay leaves

25g (1oz) unsalted butter

2 garlic cloves, crushed to a paste with a little sea salt

½ tsp crushed juniper berries

2 tsp mild curry powder or paste

1 tbsp dark muscovado sugar

450ml (¾ pint) good beef stock, boiling or hot

1 tbsp Worcestershire sauce

3 tbsp grated horseradish in vinegar, drained

16 baby Chantenay carrots, trimmed and scrubbed

175g (6oz) frozen petits pois, defrosted

salt and freshly ground black pepper

to serve

mashed or new potatoes

1. Coat the braising steaks in the seasoned flour on both sides, shaking off any excess.

2. Heat half the dripping in a frying pan to almost smoking, then fry the steaks quickly on both sides until nicely browned. Remove and set aside.

3. Add the remaining dripping to the frying pan, now over a medium heat, and fry the onions, celery, thyme and bay leaf leaves for 8–10 minutes, until the onion has softened and turned a pale golden colour.

4. Add the butter with the garlic, juniper berries, curry powder and sugar, stir to combine and cook for 2–3 minutes until aromatic. Transfer the mixture to your slow cooker, top with the steaks and stir in the remaining ingredients, except the peas. Cover and cook on low for 8–10 hours.

5. Turn the slow cooker to high, add the peas, season, then cover and cook for a further 20 minutes. Serve with mash or new potatoes.

Antony's tips
For the seasoned flour I like to add salt, pepper, a pinch of celery salt and ½ tsp English mustard powder.

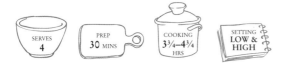

SERVES 4 · PREP 30 MINS · COOKING 3¾–4¾ HRS · SETTING LOW & HIGH

I know you're thinking, "but I don't like prunes". Nor did I, but it's funny, when you partner pork with prunes they become the perfect marriage, and the great thing about pork is that it is such good value.

Pork fillets with prune and parsley stuffing

25g (1oz) unsalted butter

2 shallots, very finely chopped

4 dried apricots, finely chopped

1 celery stick, very finely chopped

4 tbsp finely chopped parsley

2 tsp finely chopped mint

2 tbsp extra-virgin olive oil

40g (1½oz) fresh white breadcrumbs

25g (1oz) pine nuts, toasted and finely chopped

grated zest of 1 organic orange

salt and freshly ground black pepper

8 Agen prunes, stoned

2 x 225g (8oz) pork tenderloins, silverskin (shiny membrane) removed

6 slices of Parma ham

180ml (6fl oz) dry white wine

sage leaves

to serve

cabbage or green beans

mashed potato

1. Heat the butter in a frying pan, then gently cook the shallots, apricots and celery for about 10 minutes, until soft. Tip into a bowl and add the parsley, mint, half the oil, the breadcrumbs, pine nuts and orange zest. Mix together and season. Squeeze this stuffing into 8 small balls, which you put in the centre of each split prune.

2. Split the pork fillet lengthways by cutting three-quarters of the way through. Open each up like a book, then cover the cut side with cling film and bash evenly with a meat mallet or a rolling pin until the meat is about 0.5cm (¼in) thick.

3. Arrange 3 slices of slightly overlapping Parma ham on a board and place a flattened pork fillet on top, cut side up. Arrange 4 stuffed prunes down the length of the fillet, and then roll up completely, enclosing the fillet in Parma ham. Secure with 3 cocktail sticks. Repeat with the other fillet.

4. Heat the remaining oil in a frying pan and brown the fillets all over on a high heat. Remove and place in the bottom of your slow cooker.

5. Pour the wine into the frying pan, scrape and stir up any sticky bits and bring to the boil. Pour over the pork, then cover and cook on low for 3–4 hours.

6. Add the sage to the slow cooker, increase the temperature to high, cover and cook for 40 minutes, until the meat is cooked.

7. Remove the pork and carve each fillet into 4. Arrange 2 slices on each plate, spoon over the cooking juices and serve with cabbage or green beans and mashed potato.

Also try
If you wish, use chicken breasts instead of the pork, and cook for the same length of time.

SERVES 4

PREP 20 MINS

COOKING 8½–10½ HRS

SETTING LOW & HIGH

In my earlier life I was never a fan of fruit in savoury cooking, but then I discovered Morocco and fell in love with tagines. This recipe has little to do with Morocco, but it has similar influences.

Garlic and sage pork with fennel and pears

1.2kg (2lb 11oz) boneless neck or rolled shoulder of pork

1 tbsp olive oil

2 tbsp fennel seeds

1 tsp dried oregano

1 tsp dried rosemary

3 tbsp wholegrain Dijon mustard

1 tsp Maldon sea salt

1 tsp crushed black peppercorns

1 head of garlic, broken into cloves and lightly smashed with the back of a knife

1 bunch sage, tied with string

150ml (¼ pint) chicken stock

150ml (¼ pint) dry perry (pear cider)

2 tsp runny honey

2 Conference pears, peeled, cored and cut into wedges

to serve
creamy mashed potato
green vegetables

1. Tie the pork with kitchen string to create a more uniform shape. Heat the oil in a frying pan and brown the pork all over on a high heat, remove and allow to cool.

2. In a mortar and pestle or electric coffee grinder, crush the fennel, oregano and rosemary to a powder, then set aside.

3. Paint the pork all over with the mustard, then sprinkle with the fennel mix and the salt and pepper. Place the pork carefully in the slow cooker and add the garlic, sage, stock, perry and honey, then place the pears around the meat.

4. Cover and cook on low for 8–10 hours, until the meat is cooked. Remove the pork from the cooker, cover with foil and rest in a warm place while you turn the cooker to high to reduce the juices slightly. Cook, uncovered, for 25 minutes.

5. Carve the pork, then return it to the cooker for 10 minutes to warm through. Serve with the pears, the juices, some creamy mash and a green vegetable, perhaps fine green beans.

Also try
Feel free to replace the pears and perry and use instead tart eating apples, such as Cox's, and a slug of apple cider.

SERVES
4

PREP
30 MINS

MARINATE
OVER-
NIGHT

COOKING
6–7 HRS

SETTING
HIGH

All my family love this dish and its delicious balance between sweet
and pepper. Look no further for perfect comfort food on a parky
day, when your body needs a little TLC.

Spicy pork in stout

1.5kg (3lb 5oz) piece of boneless thick
    end of belly pork, skin removed

6 Kalamata olives, stoned

6 sage leaves

6 stoned prunes

6 anchovy fillets in oil, drained

2 tbsp olive oil

25g (1oz) butter

2 onions, cut into thick wedges

2 tbsp plain flour

1 can (330ml/11fl oz) Guinness or stout

300ml (½ pint) chicken stock

for the marinade

2 tsp crushed black peppercorns

1 tsp salt

2 tsp dried oregano

1 tsp soft thyme leaves

7 garlic cloves, peeled

3 tbsp soft brown sugar

2 tbsp olive oil

2 tbsp red wine vinegar

to serve

mashed potato

baby broad beans

finely chopped fresh herbs
    (eg parsley, chives)

1. Turn the pork so that the underside is uppermost on a chopping board.
Make 12 deep incisions spread evenly over the meat's surface. Wrap each
olive with a sage leaf and stuff each prune with a rolled-up anchovy fillet.
Press these into the pork incisions.

2. Put all the marinade ingredients into a mini food processor and blend
to a smooth paste. Pour half into the base of a shallow china dish, add the
pork so that it lies flat, then rub the rest of the marinade over the top. Cover
with cling film and refrigerate overnight.

3. Scrape some of the excess marinade from the pork and reserve, then roll
up the pork from one of the short ends with the "stuffed" side innermost,
and tie at intervals along its length with string.

4. Heat the oil in a frying pan over a high heat, add the pork and fry, turning,
until evenly browned, adding the butter and onions halfway through. Lift
the pork into your slow cooker.

5. Stir the flour into the pan, cook gently for 3 minutes, stirring regularly,
then mix in the remaining marinade, Guinness and stock. Bring to the boil,
scraping and stirring up the bits from the base of the pan, then tip the
mixture into the slow cooker. Cover and cook on high for 6–7 hours until the
pork is cooked and very tender.

6. Transfer the pork to a serving plate, cut into thick slices and discard the
string. Serve with spoonfuls of the Guinness sauce, mashed potato and
baby broad beans tossed with chopped fresh herbs.

Slow cooker tips
It is important that large joints of pork are cooked only on the high setting and submerged in liquid so that they cook
evenly. If you would prefer the finished sauce to be thicker, purée the onions and sauce, then tip into a wide shallow
saucepan and boil rapidly for 5 minutes or so until it has reduced to your liking.

SERVES **4**　PREP **15** MINS　COOKING **7–8** HRS　SETTING **HIGH**

This is a really useful meat recipe because, although it eats well as it is with mashed potato or a bowl of lentils, it's also a great standby for soups, salads and stews. Think of this recipe as a foundation for bigger things. You can add spuds, root vegetables, chorizo, clams, tomatoes – the choice is yours.

Poached pork shoulder

1 large onion, thinly sliced

1 carrot, thinly sliced

1 x 1.5kg (3lb 5 oz) boneless pork shoulder joint

½ bottle dry white wine

500ml (18fl oz) chicken stock

1 tsp sea salt

2 tsp finely chopped fresh ginger

1 tsp black peppercorns

4 dried chillies

1 clove

1 tbsp runny honey

1 star anise

1 head of garlic, cut in half horizontally

2 tsp coriander seeds

1 tsp cumin seeds

2 bay leaves

2 celery sticks, thinly sliced

2 tbsp roughly chopped coriander leaves

to serve

hot Puy lentils or mashed potato

Dijon mustard

1. Place the onion and carrot in your slow cooker with the pork on top. Add all the remaining ingredients.

2. Cover and cook on high for 7–8 hours until the meat is cooked. Halfway through cooking, turn the pork over. Remove the meat from the stock.

3. Serve the hot pork with lentils or mashed potatoes and some good strong mustard.

Using the stock

If serving the pork cold, allow the meat to cool in the stock. When cold, take out the meat, strain the stock through muslin and remove the fat: this is a good base for sauces or soups and can be frozen for up to 6 months.

SERVES 4–6   PREP 10 MINS   SOAK 4 HRS   COOKING 6½–8½ HRS   SETTING HIGH

With an Irish wife, many a meal has included gammon and potatoes, so ringing the changes can be a challenge. This variation was inspired by a recipe from a great chef, Phil Vickery.

Braised gammon and potatoes with a peach and Barkham Blue cheese sauce

1kg (2lb 4oz) gammon joint, soaked in cold water for 4 hours

1kg (2lb 4oz) floury potatoes, cut into 0.5cm (¼in) slices

2 onions, finely sliced

1 tbsp soft thyme leaves

salt and freshly ground black pepper

25g (1oz) butter

12 baby carrots, trimmed and scrubbed

2 bay leaves

210ml (7fl oz) chicken stock

210ml (7fl oz) peach juice

for the sauce

400g (14oz) tin peach halves in juice, drained

150ml (¼ pint) double cream

125g (4½oz) Barkham Blue or another blue cheese, crumbled

to serve

runner or French beans

1. Place the gammon in a large saucepan, cover with cold water and bring to the boil. Reduce the heat, cover with a lid and simmer for 30 minutes. Layer the potatoes and onions in the bottom of your slow cooker, sprinkle with the thyme, then season and dot the top with the butter.

2. Remove the gammon from the saucepan and nestle in the potato layers. Add the baby carrots and bay leaves. Pour in the stock and peach juice, then cover and cook on high for 6–8 hours, until the meat is cooked.

3. Meanwhile, to make the sauce, whiz the peaches in a food processor until smooth. In a small pan, gently heat the cream and cheese until melted. Stir in the peach purée and heat through. (This can be made in advance.)

4. Remove the gammon and carve. Spoon the potatoes and onions onto warm plates and arrange the meat on top. Serve with the sauce on the side and runner or French beans.

SERVES
4

PREP
15 MINS

COOKING
7 HRS

SETTING
LOW &
HIGH

Even big children love ribs and these are beautifully sticky and
flavoursome. The slow cooking produces a very tender result,
perfect for just finishing off on the barbecue.

Caramelized pork ribs with bourbon and ginger

2 racks of baby back pork ribs

240ml (8fl oz) bourbon whiskey

25g (1oz) fresh ginger, thinly sliced

4 garlic cloves

2 long red chillies

1 litre (1¾ pints) chicken stock

2 tbsp vegetable oil

for the sauce

2 garlic cloves, crushed to a paste with a
  little sea salt

2 tsp grated fresh ginger

½ tsp dried chilli flakes

115g (4oz) soft dark brown sugar

120ml (4fl oz) rice vinegar

240ml (8fl oz) good tomato ketchup

to serve

jacket potatoes

home-made apple coleslaw

1. Place the ribs in a slow cooker with the bourbon, sliced ginger, garlic, chillies and stock. Cover and cook on low for 6 hours until the meat is cooked through.

2. Remove the ribs and set aside, increase the heat to high, leave uncovered and cook the liquor for 45 minutes or until reduced by half.

3. Meanwhile, paint the cooked ribs with the oil and fry in a large frying pan over a high heat until brown all over. Set aside.

4. Preheat your grill to hot or oven to 220°C/425°F/Gas 7, or have your barbecue ready. Combine the reduced cooking juices with the sauce ingredients and paint this sauce over the ribs. Cook the ribs until nicely glazed (be careful, they burn easily), turning the ribs a couple of times and continuing to paint to build up a glaze.

5. Serve with jacket potatoes and hand-made apple coleslaw.

FOR THE APPLE COLESLAW
For the apple coleslaw: whisk together 1 garlic clove crushed to a paste with sea salt, 2 anchovy fillets in oil (drained), mashed to a paste, 120ml (4fl oz) good mayonnaise, 120ml (4fl oz) Greek yoghurt, 2 tsp Dijon mustard and 1 tbsp finely chopped dill. Set aside. Whisk 2 tbsp white wine vinegar with 2 tsp golden caster sugar and toss with ½ large Savoy cabbage, shredded. Leave for 1 hour. Fold in 2 dessert apples, core and diced, then add enough dressing to coat and mix well. Season to taste, cover and chill for 1 hour.

Also try
Replace the bourbon with 240ml (8fl oz) dark soy sauce for a less American, and more Asian, set of ribs.

Bakes

Steak and kidney pudding

see page 112

A perfect supper dish that ticks all the boxes. It's excellent with poached eggs or as an accompaniment to grilled or roast meat or fish.

Vegetable and red pepper gratin

4 rashers smoked streaky bacon, cut into lardons

25g (1oz) unsalted butter

2 leeks, shredded

½ red pepper, cored, deseeded and chopped

400g (14oz) tin sweetcorn, drained

salt and freshly ground black pepper

4 egg yolks

1 tsp English mustard powder

600ml (1 pint) double cream

½ tsp Tabasco

½ tsp Worcestershire sauce

1. Cook the bacon with the butter in a frying pan over a medium heat, for about 3 minutes until crisp. Add the leeks and red pepper and cook for a further 5 minutes, stirring occasionally. Add the sweetcorn and stir to combine. Season and put the mixture into your slow cooker.

2. In a bowl, beat together the egg yolks, mustard, cream, Tabasco and Worcestershire sauce. Season again with salt and pepper and pour over the sweetcorn mix.

3. Cover and cook on low for 2–3 hours, until a knife inserted into the centre of the gratin comes out clean.

How to check if the gratin is cooked
To check if the gratin is cooked without lifting the lid too often, see if it looks cooked, then if it does, carefully shake the slow cooker and there should be a firm wobble rather than loose liquid.

SERVES 4 | PREP 15 MINS | COOKING 4 HRS | SETTING HIGH

This is a blast from the past, very popular in the 1980s, the era of nouvelle cuisine, when you might receive six or seven stuffed vegetables as a vegetarian main course. They would have been miniature vegetables, whereas these stuffed onions are far more robust.

Onions stuffed with tomatos, garlic and mozzarella

2 large Spanish onions, whole and unpeeled

55g (2oz) fresh white breadcrumbs

2 tbsp olive oil, plus extra for greasing

3 garlic cloves, roughly chopped

4 tbsp finely chopped curly parsley

2 tbsp freshly grated Parmesan

1 tsp soft thyme leaves

salt and freshly ground black pepper

8 sun-dried tomatoes, roughly chopped

1 ball cow's mozzarella, cut into 1cm (¼in) dice

2 tbsp pine nuts

150ml (¼ pint) vegetable stock, boiling or hot

1. Cook the whole onions in boiling salted water for 15 minutes, drain and when cool enough to handle, cut in half horizontally and peel.

2. Use a melon baller or teaspoon to remove about 4 layers of onion from the centre of each half and reserve, leaving a thick layer of onion with an intact base. Slice a very small amount off the base of each onion half, so it can stand flat.

3. Meanwhile, in a mini food processor, blend together the breadcrumbs, oil, garlic, parsley, Parmesan and thyme.

4. Finely chop half of the reserved onion centres, season to taste and fold them into the breadcrumb mix with the tomatoes, mozzarella and pine nuts. Fill the hollowed-out centres of the 4 onion halves with the stuffing.

5. Lightly oil the base of your slow cooker pot, then place the stuffed onions into it. Carefully pour the stock around the onions, cover and cook on high for 4 hours, basting the onions once.

6. Remove the delicate onions to a Swiss roll tin or shallow roasting tray, then place under a preheated grill for 2–3 minutes to brown.

SERVING SUGGESTION
Serve with a leaf salad or as an accompaniment to your Sunday roast.

Risotto is always a popular standby and it does work with your slow cooker, albeit not quite as well as the stove-top method. Give it a shot – I think you'll be impressed.

Wild mushroom risotto

1.5 litres (3 pints) vegetable stock

25g (1oz) dried cèpes (porcini), soaked in hot water for 20 minutes

85g (3oz) unsalted butter

1 tbsp olive oil

1 onion, finely chopped

1 celery stick, finely chopped

1 garlic clove, finely chopped

1 carrot, finely chopped

1 thyme sprig

1 bay leaf

325g (11½oz) Arborio risotto rice

240ml (8fl oz) full-bodied red wine

225g (8oz) fresh wild mushrooms, finely sliced

85g (3oz) freshly grated Parmesan

2 tbsp finely chopped flat-leaf parsley

to serve

green salad

1. Heat the stock in a saucepan and keep warm.

2. Strain the cèpes and reserve the soaking water. Finely chop the cèpes and set aside.

3. Melt half the butter with the oil in a heavy-based saucepan over a medium heat. Add the onion, celery, garlic, carrot, thyme and bay leaf and cook for about 6–8 minutes, stirring occasionally, until the onion has softened but not browned. Add the cèpes and cook for 3–4 minutes.

4. Add the rice and stir until the grains are well coated. Add the wine, mushroom soaking liquid and two-thirds of the stock. Bring to the boil and transfer to your slow cooker, then cover and cook on low for 1½–2 hours.

5. Add the fresh mushrooms, turn the slow cooker to high, cover and cook for a further 15 minutes. Add more warm stock, if extra liquid is required to prevent the risotto drying out.

6. When the rice is cooked, fold in the remaining butter, the Parmesan and parsley. Serve with a green salad.

SERVES
4

PREP
15 MINS

COOKING
35 MINS

SETTING
LOW &
HIGH

Baked eggs have all but disappeared from domestic menus, although you occasionally see them in restaurants. They're very easy to prepare and produce a satisfying texture when cooked in the slow cooker.

Baked eggs with leek and tomato

25g (1oz) unsalted butter

225g (8oz) leeks, green discarded, white very thinly sliced

1 tsp soft thyme leaves

120ml (4fl oz) double cream

salt and freshly ground black pepper

55g (2oz) Gruyère, grated

4 large eggs

1 beefsteak tomato, cored and cut into 4 slices

2 tsp extra-virgin olive oil

to serve
crusty bread

1. Pour 2.5cm (1in) boiling water into the bottom of your slow cooker, turn to high and place an upturned plate or saucer in the bottom.

2. Grease 4 large individual ramekins with half the butter.

3. Melt the remaining butter in a frying pan and, over a medium heat, gently cook the leeks with the thyme for 5–8 minutes, stirring occasionally. Stir in half the cream, increase the heat and cook for a further 2 minutes. Season to taste.

4. Spoon the leeks into the ramekins, pushing them slightly up the sides to create a hollow in the centre. Sprinkle a little Gruyère over the leeks, then carefully break an egg into each hollow. Pour over the remaining cream and lightly season.

5. Gently place a slice of tomato over each egg, top with the remaining cheese and drizzle with the oil. Place the ramekins in your slow cooker, cover and cook on low for 30 minutes, until the whites are just setting.

6. Place the ramekins under a preheated grill for 2–3 minutes until the cheese is browned.

7. Serve as a starter or supper dish with crusty bread.

SERVES
6–8

PREP
15 MINS +
REFRIGERATE
OVERNIGHT

COOKING
4 HRS

SETTING
HIGH

Here's something a little special for a dinner party. It requires a bit of patience, but for the keen cook it's worth the effort. Do mix and match the smoked fish, for instance kipper fillets instead of smoked haddock.

Smoked fish terrine

1 tsp vegetable oil, for oiling

385g (13½oz) best long-cut smoked salmon (rather than D cut)

450g (1lb) undyed smoked haddock fillets, skin removed

450g (1lb) hot-smoked salmon fillets, skin removed

2 eggs, lightly beaten

120ml (4fl oz) soured cream or crème fraîche

2 tsp snipped chives

2 tsp lilliput (extra-fine) capers, drained

2 tsp finely chopped dill

2 tsp horseradish cream

salt and freshly ground black pepper

to serve

toast

1. Pour 2.5cm (1in) warm water into the bottom of your slow cooker, turn it onto high and place an upturned plate or saucer in the bottom.

2. Lightly oil a 1kg (2lb 4oz) loaf tin or terrine and line with cling film, allowing a 7.5cm (3in) overhang on each side.

3. Line the terrine with the smoked salmon slices, leaving a similar overhang to cover the top when the terrine is full.

4. Put the smoked haddock fillet on a board next to the terrine and cut to length to fill the terrine. Wrap this rectangle of smoked haddock fillet in the remaining smoked salmon.

5. Cut the leftover smoked haddock into 1cm (½in) chunks and place in a bowl. Flake the hot-smoked salmon into another bowl and set both aside.

6. In a third bowl, mix together the eggs, cream, chives, capers, dill and horseradish. Season well. Spoon half the mix into the diced haddock, and the remaining half into the flaked salmon. Stir each to combine.

7. Spoon the smoked haddock mix into the bottom of the terrine, top with the smoked-salmon-wrapped haddock, then finally top with the hot-smoked salmon mix. Level the surface and fold the overhanging smoked salmon over the top, then the cling film. Seal well.

8. Place the terrine in the slow cooker. Carefully add more boiling water to come halfway up the sides of the terrine. Cover and cook on high for about 4 hours, until a skewer inserted in the terrine comes out clean.

9. Remove the terrine and place 2 or 3 cans on top to compress the filling. Leave to cool, then chill overnight in your fridge. Lift the terrine out of the mould with the help of the cling film, unwrap and cut into thick slices. Serve with toast.

This is really nice presented at the table in its own Kilner jar. Cooking the terrine in the jar sterilizes it and so it will keep a lot longer than if you used a terrine mould or loaf tin.

Chicken, pork, apple and walnut terrine

1 tbsp olive oil

1 onion, finely chopped

3 garlic cloves, crushed to a paste with a little sea salt

2 tsp soft thyme leaves

1 chicken breast, finely chopped

325g (11½oz) cleaned chicken livers, ¾ finely chopped and ¼ cut in half

2 rashers smoked streaky bacon, finely chopped

300g (10½oz) coarse pork mince

1 egg, beaten

3 tbsp Calvados or brandy

55g (2oz) fresh white breadcrumbs

3 pickled walnuts, drained and diced

2 tsp soft green peppercorns in brine, drained

1 tsp Maldon sea salt

1 Cox's or Granny Smith apple, peeled, cored, and diced

1. In a frying pan, heat the olive oil and gently cook the onion, garlic and thyme for 8 minutes, until softened but not coloured. Allow to cool.

2. In a bowl, combine the chicken breast, finely chopped chicken livers, bacon and pork mince. Beat together the egg and Calvados and add to the meat mix with the onion and all the remaining ingredients, except the halved chicken livers. Stir well.

3. Divide half the meat mix between 2 x 500ml (16½fl oz) sterilized Kilner jars. Press it down and top with the halved chicken livers, then the remaining meat mix, press it down again and smooth the surface. Seal the lids and place the jars in your slow cooker, pour boiling water three-quarters of the way up the sides of the jars, cover and cook on high for 3–4 hours until the meat is cooked and the juices are almost clear. Remove and cool.

4. Store in the fridge until ready to eat. Unopened, these terrines should last at least a couple of weeks.

SERVING SUGGESTION
Serve with hot country bread, cornichons, small chunks of Parmesan and a little salad.

How to sterilize Kilner jars
See page 215 for details.

SERVES 4   PREP 20 MINS   COOKING 2¼ HRS   SETTING HIGH

There aren't many dishes that win over most palates, but fish pie is one such dish that does, whether it be with a potato or pastry topping, or in this case melting cheesy breadcrumbs.

A not-so-classic fish pie

225g (8oz) skinless undyed smoked haddock fillets, cut into bite-sized pieces

225g (8oz) skinless salmon fillets, cut into bite-sized pieces

2 tbsp cornflour

salt and freshly ground black pepper

115g (4oz) frozen petits pois, defrosted

115g (4oz) tin sweetcorn, drained

115g (4oz) smooth cream cheese

1 tbsp finely chopped dill

1 tsp English mustard powder

75ml (2½fl oz) single cream

75ml (2½fl oz) milk

1 tbsp horseradish cream

175g (6oz) cooked, peeled North Atlantic prawns

25g (1oz) fresh or dried white breadcrumbs

2 tbsp finely chopped flat-leaf parsley

1 tbsp olive oil

1 tsp sweet paprika

4 tbsp grated Parmesan

2 tsp snipped chives

55g (2oz) Cheddar, grated

to serve

English salad of lettuce, tomato and cucumber with hard-boiled eggs

1. Combine the haddock and salmon in a bowl and toss thoroughly with the cornflour. Season. Mix with the peas and sweetcorn.

2. In another bowl, beat together the cream cheese, dill, mustard, cream and milk. Fold in the horseradish cream and the fish and vegetable mixture. Spoon into your slow cooker, cover and cook on high for 2 hours.

3. Fold in the prawns, cover and cook on high for 10 minutes.

4. Meanwhile, in a food processor, blend together the breadcrumbs with the parsley, oil, paprika, Parmesan and chives until the crumbs become pale green. Tip into a bowl and combine with the Cheddar.

5. Remove the ceramic cooking pot from the slow cooker, sprinkle over the cheesy crumbs and glaze the crust under a preheated grill for about 5 minutes until golden. Serve with an English salad.

SERVES
4

PREP
45 MINS

COOKING
5½–6½ HRS

SETTING
LOW & HIGH

Turkey is one of the healthy proteins, but it can be a bit bland. It never need be again, once you've tried this recipe! Although the ingredients seem long, many are used in both parts of the recipe, so it's not as daunting as it first seems.

Turkey meatballs with tomato rice pilaf

for the meatballs

500g (1lb 2oz) minced turkey

grated zest of 1 organic orange

4 ripe tomatoes, finely diced

2 garlic cloves, crushed to a paste

1 onion, coarsely grated

8 tbsp finely chopped flat-leaf parsley

1 tbsp finely chopped coriander leaves

55g (2oz) fresh white breadcrumbs

1 egg, lightly beaten

1 tbsp Worcestershire sauce

pinch of ground allspice

½ tsp each ground coriander and cumin

¼ tsp ground fennel

1 tbsp malt vinegar

3 tbsp grated Parmesan

½ tsp salt and ¼ tsp black pepper

1½ tbsp vegetable oil

for the pilaf

1½ tbsp vegetable oil

1 onion, coarsely grated

2 garlic cloves, crushed to a paste

pinch of freshly ground black pepper

pinch of ground allspice

½ tsp each ground coriander and cumin

¼ tsp ground fennel

2 carrots, finely chopped or grated

200g (7oz) tin chopped tomatoes

750ml (1¼ pints) chicken stock, boiling

175g (6oz) basmati rice, rinsed

115g (4oz) baby spinach

½ bunch coriander, roughly chopped

40g (1½oz) cashew nuts, chopped

2 tbsp red wine vinegar

½ bunch flat-leaf parsley, chopped

1. To make the meatballs: in a bowl, combine the turkey mince, orange zest, tomatoes, garlic, onion, herbs, breadcrumbs, egg, Worcestershire sauce, spices, malt vinegar and Parmesan.

2. Season with the salt and pepper, then mould into golf-ball-sized balls. Place a non-stick frying pan over a medium to high heat and add the oil. Brown the turkey balls on all sides. Remove to a plate and set aside.

3. To make the pilaf: heat the oil in the frying pan, then sweat the onion and garlic for 6–8 minutes. Add the spices and carrots and cook for 5 minutes, stirring occasionally. Pour in the chopped tomatoes and half the stock. Transfer to your slow cooker.

4. Add the meatballs to the sauce, cover and cook on low for 4–5 hours until the meatballs are cooked through.

5. Add the remaining stock and the rice, stir to combine, turn the slow cooker to high and cook, covered, for 40 minutes.

6. Lay the spinach and the coriander on the surface and cook for 40 minutes, until the spinach has wilted. Stir to combine, then fold in the cashew nuts and the red wine vinegar. Season to taste. Serve sprinkled with the parsley and with a green salad or broccoli, peas or beans.

Slow cooker tips
Try these meatballs with your favourite tomato sauce recipe. Just add to the slow cooker, cover and cook on low for 4–5 hours, until the meat is cooked.

If you make the pilaf on its own, cook it on high for 1½–2 hours.

SERVES
6–8

PREP
30 MINS

COOKING
6 HRS
4.5 L
LARGE POT

SETTING
HIGH

Who can resist a traditional steak and kidney pudding? It came top in a recent BBC poll of the best-loved British dishes. The beauty of this dish is the ability to change the filling, for instance reducing the quantity of meat and adding more vegetables.

Steak and kidney pudding

750g (1lb 10oz) chuck steak or blade steak, cut into 2.5cm (1in) cubes

225g (8oz) ox kidney, cut into 2.5cm (1in) cubes

2 small onions, finely chopped

large pinch of celery salt

1 tsp soft thyme leaves

salt and freshly ground black pepper

150ml (¼ pint) fresh beef stock (from a carton is fine)

1 tsp English mustard powder

1 tbsp tomato purée

1 tbsp Worcestershire sauce

unsalted butter, for greasing

2 tbsp plain flour

for the suet pastry

400g (14oz) self-raising flour, plus extra for dusting

½ tsp salt

200g (7oz) shredded beef or vegetarian suet

freshly ground black pepper

300ml (½ pint) cold water

to serve

mashed potatoes

buttered peas

1. Place the steak and kidney in a large bowl. Stir in the onion, celery salt, thyme and seasoning. Toss together lightly and set to one side, or cover with cling film and chill for up to 24 hours to allow the flavours to develop.

2. Meanwhile, mix together the stock , tomato purée and Worcestershire sauce. Butter a 1.75 litre (3 pint) pudding basin.

3. To make the suet pastry: sift the flour and salt into a large bowl. Add the suet and season with pepper. Lightly mix and then add the water, a little at a time, cutting through the dough with a round-bladed knife, as if you were making scones. Use your hands to form the soft pastry.

4. Roll out on a lightly floured work surface into a round disc roughly 1cm (½in) thick. Cut out a wedge (one-quarter) of the pastry to within 2.5cm (1in) of the centre and set aside. Lift the remaining pastry into the basin and overlap the cut edges, damp with a little water and press together, so that the basin is completely lined. Leave at least 1cm (½in) overhanging the rim.

5. Add the flour to the steak and kidney mixture and stir gently to combine. Place batches of the meat mixture into a sieve (over a bowl) and shake to remove any excess flour. Spoon into the lined basin, being careful not to press it down, then pour in enough beef stock mixture to come nearly two-thirds up to the top of the basin, but not covering the meat completely.

6. Roll out the reserved pastry into a circle 2.5cm (1in) larger than the top of the basin and 1cm (½in) thick. Dampen the edges of the pastry lining the basin, place the lid over the filling and press the 2 edges together to seal. Trim off any excess pastry and make 2 small slits in the centre of the lid.

7. Cover with a double layer of buttered foil, pleated in the centre to allow for expansion. Secure the foil with string, making a handle to lift the basin. Place on an upturned plate in the slow cooker and pour in boiling water to come two-thirds of the way up the side of the basin. Cover and cook on high for 6 hours until cooked, topping up with boiling water occasionally.

8. Cut the string and remove the foil. Serve with mashed potatoes and buttered peas.

Stews

A stew of fish in a saffron broth

see page 122

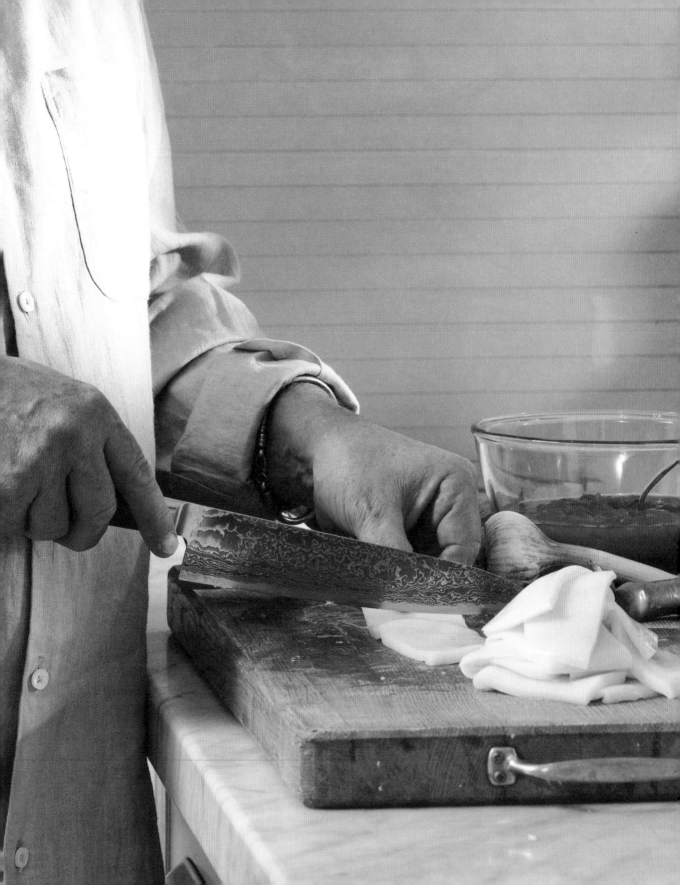

SERVES 4

PREP 15 MINS

COOKING 5¼–6¼ HRS

SETTING LOW & HIGH

This adds a little flavour of the Mediterranean to your menu. It's great as a vegetarian dish on its own or as an accompaniment to fish, poultry or meat.

Italian leek stew

1 tbsp olive oil

1kg (2lb 4oz) leeks, cut into 3cm (1¼in) chunks and washed

1 onion, finely chopped

2 garlic cloves, finely chopped

½ tsp cayenne pepper

55g (2oz) Kalamata olives, stoned and roughly chopped

400g (14oz) tin chopped tomatoes

400g (14oz) tin borlotti beans, drained and rinsed

1 ball cow's mozzarella, finely diced

12 large basil leaves, torn into small pieces

salt and freshly ground black pepper

to serve
brown rice

1. Heat the oil in a large frying pan over a medium heat and add the leeks, onion, garlic and cayenne. Fry, stirring occasionally, until lightly browned. Transfer to your slow cooker.

2. Add the olives and tomatoes, plus 180ml (6fl oz) water and the beans, then stir to combine. Cook on low for 5–6 hours.

3. Turn the slow cooker to high and stir in the mozzarella and basil. Cover and cook for a further 15 minutes.

4. Season to taste and serve with brown rice.

Slow cooker tips
You can cook this for up to 8 hours before the leeks become past their best.

SERVES 4 · PREP 15 MINS · COOKING 6–8 HRS · SETTING LOW

This is based loosely on mushrooms à la grecque: it's delicious as part of a meze, as a vegetarian dish served with couscous or rice, or even as a vegetable with grilled or roast meats.

Button mushroom and tomato stew

450g (1lb) button mushrooms

juice and grated zest of 1 unwaxed or organic lemon

2 tbsp olive oil

3 garlic cloves, crushed to a paste with a little sea salt

4–5 shallots, finely chopped

1 tbsp coriander seeds

1 tbsp fennel seeds

1 bay leaf

400g (14oz) tin chopped tomatoes

1 large glass dry white wine

1 red chilli

1 tbsp tomato purée

1 tbsp caster sugar

salt and freshly ground black pepper

to garnish
1 tbsp finely chopped flat-leaf parsley

to serve
basmati rice or penne
Greek yoghurt

1. Toss the mushrooms with the lemon juice and zest in a bowl.

2. In a deep frying pan, heat a generous slug of the olive oil, add the garlic and shallots and cook them gently for 8–10 minutes. Transfer them to your slow cooker.

3. Add the remaining ingredients, except the parsley, stir to combine, cover and cook on low for 6–8 hours.

4. Season to taste and garnish with the parsley.

SERVING SUGGESTION
For a simple lunch, this is good with basmati rice or penne. It's excellent with a dollop of Greek yoghurt too.

SERVES
4

PREP
15 MINS

COOKING
2 HRS

SETTING
LOW &
HIGH

Not many of us think about treating fish in the same manner as a piece of meat, but if you use a robust fish, such as a yellowfin tuna, salmon or even mackerel, you will find this recipe works a treat.

Fillets of fish in a smoky barbecue sauce

4 x 200g (7oz) firm fish fillets
salt and freshly ground black pepper

for the barbecue sauce
1 tbsp rapeseed or vegetable oil
1 onion, finely chopped
2 garlic cloves, crushed to a paste with a little sea salt
2 tsp fennel seeds
1 tsp chilli powder
2 tsp smoked paprika
1 tbsp soy sauce
2 tbsp soft dark brown sugar
2 tbsp sherry vinegar
2 tbsp mild American mustard
150ml (¼ pint) good tomato ketchup

to serve
potato wedges

1. Heat the oil in a frying pan and cook the onion and garlic over a gentle heat for 8–10 minutes, until the onions have softened but not coloured.

2. Stir in the fennel seeds, chilli powder, paprika, soy sauce, sugar, vinegar, mustard and ketchup. Heat gently until boiling, then carefully pour into your slow cooker.

3. Cover and cook the barbecue sauce on low for 1 hour, then increase to high, add the fish fillets and push under the surface of the sauce. Cover and cook for 1 hour, until the fish is tender and cooked.

4. Season to taste. Serve with fried or oven-baked potato wedges.

Also try
Do try cooking chicken thighs, instead of the fish, in this sauce. Add the chicken to the sauce in the slow cooker at the end of step 2, cover and cook on low for 6–8 hours until the meat is thoroughly cooked.

SERVES
6

PREP
10 MINS

COOKING
4¼ HRS

SETTING
LOW &
HIGH

I love a good soupy fish stew and this one is a favourite. Fear not that the fish selection is too onerous. Just remember the three types of fish and their cooking times and the recipe is immediately simplified: squid and octopus for at least 4 hours on low; fish 1¼–1½ hours on low; shellfish 15–20 minutes on high.

A stew of fish in a saffron broth

1 litre (1¾ pints) dashi or fish stock

pinch of saffron strands

4 tbsp each olive oil and sesame oil

2 shallots, finely diced

2 garlic cloves, crushed to a paste with a little sea salt

2 tbsp roughly chopped coriander root or stems

5cm (2in) piece of fresh ginger, grated

2 red chillies, deseeded and diced

300ml (½ pint) dry white wine

2 bay leaves

2 dried strips of orange peel

900g (2lb) baby squid, cleaned

225g (8oz) monkfish fillet, cut into 2.5cm (1in) dice

115g (4oz) red mullet fillets (left whole)

900g (2lb) small mussels

900g (2lb) small clams

85g (3oz) sugar snap peas, topped and tailed

8 spring onions, cut into 2.5cm (1in) pieces

1 courgette, thinly sliced

8 cherry tomatoes, halved

salt and freshly ground black pepper

to serve

crusty bread

salad of Baby Gem or heart lettuce

1. Place the dashi or stock and saffron in a bowl to infuse for 15 minutes.

2. Heat the oils in a large frying pan, add the shallots, garlic, coriander root, ginger and chillies and cook for about 6 minutes, until softened but not browned. Spoon into your slow cooker, then add the white wine, bay leaves, orange peel, squid and saffron broth. Cover and cook on low for 2½ hours, then add the monkfish and mullet, cover again and cook on low for a further 1¼ hours.

3. Meanwhile, clean the mussels and clams, discarding any that do not close when tapped against the sink.

4. Turn the slow cooker to high and add the mussels, clams, sugar snap peas, spring onions, courgette and cherry tomatoes and cook for a further 20 minutes. Discard any mussels or clams that haven't opened. Season the stew to taste.

5. Pour into a large, warm soup tureen and serve with crusty bread and a large bowl of salad.

Choosing fish
Try to buy sustainably caught fish wherever possible.

SERVES 4

PREP 25 MINS

COOKING 4½–6½ HRS

SETTING LOW & HIGH

The Spanish love fish and consequently it fetches a much higher price in their markets than fish does in the UK. I'm never sure why we don't eat more fish; we do after all live on an island. On average we eat less than one portion per week and then wonder why we're not a particularly healthy population.

A robust Spanish fish and red pepper stew

3 tbsp good olive oil

2 onions, finely chopped

4 garlic cloves, crushed to a paste with a little sea salt

1 tbsp harissa paste

90ml (3fl oz) dry white wine

400g (14oz) tin chopped tomatoes

2 bay leaves

¼ tsp dried chilli flakes

1½ tsp sweet paprika

450g (1lb) floury potatoes, cut into 5cm (2in) dice

1 fennel bulb, tough outer layer removed, roughly chopped

1 red pepper, deseeded and cut into 2.5cm (1in) pieces

1 yellow pepper, cored, deseeded and cut into 2.5cm (1in) pieces

325g (11½oz) sustainable tuna, cut into 2.5cm (1in) pieces

325g (11½oz) hake or sustainable cod fillet, cut into 2.5cm (1in) pieces

salt and freshly ground black pepper

to serve

crusty bread

1. Heat the olive oil in a saucepan, add the onions and garlic and cook gently for 8–10 minutes until the onions have softened but not coloured. Add the harissa, white wine, tomatoes, bay leaves, chilli and paprika and bring slowly to the boil. Pour carefully into the slow cooker.

2. Add the potatoes, fennel and peppers, stir to combine, then cover and cook on low for 4–6 hours, until the potatoes are tender.

3. Turn the slow cooker to high and stir in the fish pieces. Cover and cook for 30 minutes until the fish is cooked.

4. Season to taste and serve with crusty bread.

SERVES 4 · PREP 45 MINS · COOKING 6–8 HRS · SETTING LOW

**Forget the days of thrashing octopus on the rocks to tenderize it –
a few days in the freezer works just as well.**

Greek octopus stew

1kg (2lb 4oz) octopus, cleaned, frozen for 3 days and defrosted

3 tbsp olive oil

2 large Spanish onions, roughly chopped

6 garlic cloves, finely chopped

2 bay leaves

1 tsp finely chopped oregano leaves

1 cinnamon stick

4 cloves

115g (4oz) sultanas

6 turns of freshly ground black pepper

115g (4oz) pine nuts, toasted

1 tbsp tomato purée

1 tbsp anchovy essence

180ml (6fl oz) dry red wine

90ml (3fl oz) *Punt e Mes* or red vermouth

3 tbsp extra-virgin olive oil

salt and freshly ground black pepper

to serve

long-grain rice

pappardelle

1. Put the octopus in a saucepan and cover with cold water. Bring to the boil and simmer for 30 minutes. Drain and wash thoroughly in cold water. Cut the octopus into bite-sized pieces and set aside.

2. Put the olive oil in a frying pan over a medium heat. Add the onion, garlic, bay leaves and oregano and cook for 10 minutes, until the onion has softened but not coloured.

3. Transfer to your slow cooker and add the octopus, cinnamon, cloves, sultanas, black pepper, pine nuts, tomato purée and anchovy essence, then stir to combine. Add 210ml (7fl oz) water, red wine, *Punt e Mes* and extra-virgin olive oil. Cover and cook on low for 6–8 hours until the octopus is cooked and tender.

4. If you want the sauce to be thicker, strain the stew through a colander placed over a large bowl. Place the octopus mixture in a warm bowl and cover with foil to keep warm. Tip the strained sauce into a saucepan and boil vigorously, until reduced to your liking. Season to taste, return the octopus mix to the pan and stir to combine.

5. Serve with rice or pappardelle.

SERVES
4–6

PREP
20 MINS

COOKING
6½–7½
HRS

SETTING
LOW &
HIGH

Rabbit has faded in popularity over the years, which is a shame because it has much more flavour that most chickens. But who am I to say? If you prefer chicken, then go for it: I would use drumsticks in this recipe.

Rabbit with fennel, peppers and chicory

4 tbsp extra-virgin olive oil

1 medium onion, finely chopped

1 tsp finely chopped rosemary leaves

2 garlic cloves, finely diced

1 bay leaf

1 large head of fennel, tough outer layer removed and cut into 8 wedges through the root end

2 heads of chicory, halved lengthways

1 large red pepper, roasted, peeled and cut into 6 lengthways, seeds discarded

1 large orange pepper, roasted, peeled and cut into 6 lengthways, seeds discarded

1 tsp dried chilli flakes

1kg (2lb 4oz) rabbit pieces on the bone

400ml (13½fl oz) chicken stock

115g (4oz) frozen peas, defrosted

1 tbsp finely chopped mint

2 tbsp coarsely chopped flat-leaf parsley

to serve
creamy mashed potato

1. Heat the oil in a frying pan over a medium heat and cook the onion, rosemary, garlic and bay leaf for about 8 minutes, until the onions are soft and translucent. Add the fennel wedges and the chicory and cook for a further 8 minutes, turning gently, until the fennel and chicory have taken on a little colour. Tip into the slow cooker.

2. Add the peppers, chilli, rabbit and stock. Stir to combine. Cover with the lid and cook on slow for 6–7 hours until the meat is cooked.

3. Increase the heat to high and add the peas, mint and parsley. Stir to combine and then cook, uncovered, for 20 minutes.

4. Serve with creamy mashed potato.

Also try
You could also cook hare pieces or diced venison or venison medallion steaks using the same cooking times.

SERVES
4

PREP
40 MINS

MARINATE
2 HRS

COOKING
1 HR

HOB

Rabbit can have a tendency to be dry so gentle cooking is crucial either in a covered pan on the hob or gently bubbling in a slow cooker. Flavoured here with pancetta, garlic, allspice and wine, this dish tells a story of rural Italian cooking.

Rabbit with rosemary

120ml (4fl oz) olive oil

2 leeks, finely chopped

2 carrots, finely chopped

2 celery sticks, finely chopped

2 bay leaves

4 dried red chillies

1.5 kg (3lb 5oz) rabbit, jointed, or 8 hind legs, sinews removed

salt and freshly ground black pepper

175g (6oz) pancetta, diced, or smoked streaky bacon, cut into lardons

6 garlic cloves, peeled

1 tsp ground allspice

25g (1oz) plain flour

450ml (¾ pint) red wine

300ml (½ pint) fresh chicken stock (from a carton is fine)

2 tbsp finely chopped rosemary leaves

to serve

mashed potato or pappardelle

buttered peas (optional)

1. Place the olive oil, leeks, carrots, celery, bay leaves and chillies in a non-metallic bowl. Add the rabbit and season generously, then stir to combine. Cover with cling film and leave to marinate in the fridge for at least 2 hours but ideally for 24 hours, stirring a couple of times.

2. Put a large heavy-based casserole over a high heat. Remove the rabbit from the marinade, brushing off the vegetables, and add to the pan in batches. Fry for about 10 minutes until nicely browned all over, turning regularly. Transfer to a plate.

3. Remove the bay leaves from the marinade and reserve, then remove and discard the chillies. Add the pancetta to the casserole and cook for 6–8 minutes to release the fat, then add all the marinated vegetable mixture and garlic. Cook for about 10 minutes over a medium heat, stirring occasionally, until the vegetables are lightly golden and just tender.

4. Stir the allspice and flour into the pan and cook for 1–2 minutes, being careful not to let the flour catch on the bottom. Gradually pour in the wine, stirring constantly, then turn up the heat and boil for a few moments.

5. Pour in the stock and stir to combine, then turn down the heat and add the browned rabbit pieces, reserved bay leaves and the rosemary. Cover and simmer for about 45 minutes, until the rabbit is cooked and completely tender. Season to taste.

6. Serve straight from the casserole with bowls of mashed potato or pappardelle, and buttered peas, if you like.

To make this in a slow cooker
At step 5, instead of simmering the stew on the hob, you can transfer it to a slow cooker, cover and cook for 6–8 hours on low, until the rabbit is cooked.

SERVES
4

PREP
20 MINS

COOKING
6½ HRS

SETTING
LOW &
HIGH

I love pork. I love the flavour pork fat gives to a stew. This is real country fare, no airs or graces, towers or foams, just good honest cooking.

Duck stew with white beans

2 tbsp duck fat

2 onions, finely diced

1 carrot, finely diced

1 celery stick, finely diced

8 garlic cloves, peeled

2 tsp tomato purée

400g (14oz) tin chopped tomatoes

180ml (6fl oz) Martini Extra Dry

2 x 400g (14oz) tins cannellini beans,
  drained and rinsed

225g (8oz) rind from the pork belly, cut
  into 0.5cm (¼in) dice (optional)

225g (8oz) pork belly, blanched in
  boiling water for 10 minutes, drained
  and cut into lardons

2 thyme sprigs

2 bay leaves

450ml (¾ pint) chicken stock or water

4 duck confit legs, skin removed,
  meat shredded or diced

salt and freshly ground white pepper

to serve
buttered cabbage or spinach
crusty bread

1. Melt the duck fat in a frying pan over a medium heat, then fry the onions, carrot, celery and garlic for 6–8 minutes, until golden brown. Mash the garlic cloves with the back of a fork. Add the tomato purée, tomatoes and Martini, stir to combine, then transfer to your slow cooker.

2. Mix in the beans, diced pork rind, if using, pork belly lardons, thyme and bay leaves. Add the chicken stock, cover and cook on low for 6 hours, until the meat is cooked.

3. Turn the slow cooker to high, add the duck and cook for 20 minutes.

4. Season to taste. Serve with buttered cabbage or spinach and crusty fresh bread.

This is a good, old-fashioned chicken stew with a creamy finish. You can use rabbit or pork and a host of root vegetables, if you wish, in a fricassee, but I've stuck with tradition, using just baby onions and button mushrooms, and tomatoes to garnish.

Chicken, mushroom and onion fricassee

2 tbsp vegetable oil

8 chicken thighs, skin on

25g (1oz) unsalted butter

24 pickling onions, peeled

2 garlic cloves, finely chopped

225g (8oz) button mushrooms

3 tbsp plain flour

1 tsp sweet paprika

180ml (6fl oz) dry white wine

600ml (1 pint) good chicken stock, boiling

1 thyme sprig

1 bay leaf

120ml (4fl oz) double cream

2 tomatoes, deseeded and diced

4 tbsp finely chopped flat-leaf parsley

1 tsp finely chopped tarragon

salt and freshly ground black pepper

to serve

green vegetable

new potatoes

1. Put the oil in a large frying pan over a high heat and fry the chicken thighs until golden all over. Remove and set aside.

2. Add the butter to the same pan, lower the heat to medium and cook the onions, garlic and mushrooms until golden – you may have to do this in batches – then set aside.

3. Add the flour and paprika to the fat in the frying pan and stir to combine. Cook gently for 3 minutes, until the roux is lightly browned.

4. Pour in the wine and stir vigorously, loosening any bits stuck to the bottom of the pan, until emulsified. Slowly add a ladleful of stock at a time, whisking between each addition, and bring to a simmer. Pour into your slow cooker pot.

5. Fold in the onions and mushrooms, chicken, thyme and bay leaf. Cover and cook on low for 6–7 hours, until the chicken is thoroughly cooked.

6. Using a slotted spoon, remove the chicken and vegetables to a warm dish, cover loosely in foil and set aside.

7. To make the sauce in the slow cooker, fold in the double cream, tomatoes, parsley and tarragon, cover and cook on high for 15 minutes. Season to taste.

8. Pour the sauce over the chicken and vegetables, and serve with your favourite green vegetable and new potatoes.

Also try
Try this dish with rabbit rear legs or shoulder of pork.

SERVES
4

PREP
45 MINS

COOKING
8 HRS

SETTING
LOW &
HIGH

This is a great casserole for a cold day with a real depth of flavour provided by the fruit. You can substitute beef for the venison if you are not too keen on game, but I'm sure that once you've tried this recipe it will become one of your one-bowl favourites.

1kg (2lb 4oz) stewing venison, cut into 3cm (1¼in) cubes

4 tbsp seasoned flour, for dusting

2 tbsp vegetable oil or beef dripping

175g (6oz) smoked streaky bacon, diced

2 celery sticks, finely chopped

1 large onion, finely chopped

2 garlic cloves, finely chopped

2 thyme sprigs

2 tbsp redcurrant jelly

210ml (7fl oz) red wine

450ml (¾ pint) game or beef stock

90ml (3fl oz) port

1 tbsp Worcestershire sauce

12 stoned prunes

55g (2oz) dried cherries

55g (2oz) dried cranberries

200g (7oz) chestnuts, precooked and peeled

100g (3½oz) button mushrooms

2 bay leaves

grated zest of 1 organic orange

1 tbsp tomato purée

handful flat-leaf parsley, chopped

for the dumplings

150g (5½oz) plain flour

1 tsp salt

½ rounded tsp baking powder

85g (3oz) shredded beef or vegetarian suet

1 tbsp olive oil

2 tsp horseradish cream

3 tsp finely chopped flat-leaf parsley

3 tbsp snipped chives

100ml (3½fl oz) milk

melted butter, for brushing

Winter venison in a bowl with herb dumplings

1. Toss the venison in the seasoned flour.

2. Put the oil in a frying pan over a high heat and brown the venison all over – you may need to do this in batches. Remove with a slotted spoon and set aside.

3. In the same pan, add the bacon, celery, onion, garlic and thyme, then soften over a medium heat for 8–10 minutes without browning. Tip into a bowl with the venison, add the remaining casserole ingredients, except the parsley, and toss to combine. Tip into your slow cooker, cover and cook on low for 7 hours, until the meat is cooked.

4. Meanwhile, 1½ hours before the end of the cooking time, make the dumplings. Sift the flour, salt and baking powder into a large bowl. Add the suet. Make a well in the centre and add the olive oil, horseradish and herbs, pour in a little of the milk, then mix with a fork to form a soft dough, adding more milk as necessary. Place the dough on a lightly floured surface and knead for 2 minutes. Divide and shape into 12 dumplings.

5. After 7 hours, turn up the slow cooker to high. Season the casserole with pepper, stir to combine, then place the dumplings on the surface. Brush each dumpling with a little melted butter. Cover and cook for 50–60 minutes, until the dumplings have risen.

6. Allow to rest for 5 minutes, then skim off any fat that has risen to the surface. To serve, sprinkle with the parsley.

SERVES
4

PREP
10 MINS

MARINATE
2 HRS

COOKING
7½–8½ HRS

SETTING
LOW & HIGH

Chickpeas are often part of a vegetarian's staple diet, but they are also a great addition to meat stews as they are a great vehicle for delicious flavours. Feel free to add more vegetables to the lamb, especially green ones, towards the end of the cooking time.

Pot-roasted lamb with chickpeas, sweet potatoes and spices

800g (1lb 12oz) boneless leg of lamb, cut into 2.5cm (1in) dice

salt

2 tbsp vegetable oil

2 sweet potatoes, cut into 2.5cm (1in) chunks

400g (14oz) tin whole tomatoes

400g (14oz) tin chickpeas, drained and rinsed

450ml (¾ pint) lamb or chicken stock

3–4 tsp garam masala

2 handfuls spinach

115g (4oz) frozen peas, defrosted

for the marinade

3 tsp ground turmeric

2 tsp chilli powder

2 tsp ground cumin

2 tbsp ground coriander

2 bay leaves

4–6 medium green chillies

3 medium onions, finely chopped

6–8 garlic cloves, finely chopped

1cm (½in) piece of fresh ginger, finely chopped

3 tbsp mustard oil

1 tsp caster sugar

to serve

basmati rice

1. Mix the lamb with all the marinade ingredients in a large bowl. Add a little salt to taste. Cover with cling film and leave for at least 2 hours at room temperature to marinate (or for 24 hours in the fridge).

2. In a heavy-bottomed casserole, heat the vegetable oil to smoking, reduce the heat to medium, then add the meat and all the marinade ingredients. Stir fry for 12–15 minutes until brown all over but not scorched. Add to your slow cooker.

3. Add the sweet potatoes, tomatoes, chickpeas and stock. Stir to mix well. Cover and cook on low for 7–8 hours, until the meat is cooked.

4. Stir in the garam masala, spinach and peas, turn to high and cook, uncovered, for 20 minutes. Serve with steamed basmati rice.

SERVES 4

PREP 15 MINS

COOKING 2½ HRS

OVEN

We tend to forget about old classics. Not many dishes can touch the flavours of a Lancashire hotpot. Don't be put off by the idea of end of neck lamb chops as after the long slow cooking the meat is so meltingly soft it can be easily forked away from the bones.

Lancashire hotpot

1kg (2lb 4oz) end-of-neck mutton or lamb chops

4 lamb kidneys, skinned, halved horizontally and the core (the fatty white half moon inside) removed

salt and freshly ground black pepper

1 tbsp vegetable oil

55g (2oz) unsalted butter

1kg (2lb 4oz) floury potatoes, peeled and cut into 8mm ⅓in) slices

3 onions, finely sliced

2 thyme sprigs

2 bay leaves

1 tbsp caster sugar

450ml (¾ pint) lamb stock

1. Preheat the oven to 160°C/325°F/Gas 3. Season all the chops and kidneys with salt and plenty of pepper. Heat the oil in a frying pan over a high heat and brown the chops and kidneys all over, then set aside.

2. Butter the bottom of a heavy-based casserole dish with a quarter of the butter.

3. Place an overlapping layer of potatoes in the bottom of the casserole. Top this with the chops, kidney halves and onions. Tuck in the thyme sprigs and bay leaves. Season with extra salt and pepper and add the sugar.

4. Finish with the remaining potato slices, slightly overlapping each slice. Pour in the stock carefully so that it doesn't cover the top layer of potato.

5. Melt the remaining butter and brush the top of the potatoes with it. Cover the casserole with a lid and pop in the oven for 2 hours, then remove the lid, increase the heat to 200°C/400°F/Gas 6 and cook for a further 30 minutes or until the potatoes are golden brown and the meat cooked.

SERVING SUGGESTION
This is a one-pot meal, but traditionally you might serve it with pickled red cabbage on the side.

To make this in a slow cooker
If you would prefer to use your slow cooker, you can cook this for 8–10 hours on low, then brown under a hot grill. Make sure the stock is boiling hot when you add it and that your slow cooker is large enough.

SERVES 6–8 | PREP 30 MINS | MARINATE OVERNIGHT | COOKING 4 HRS | OVEN

Transform ordinary chuck or blade steak into this classic French casserole. Begin by marinating the night before you need it in a mixture of red burgundy, thyme and garlic then slowly casserole so that the beef becomes incredibly tender, moist and full of flavour.

Beef bourguignon

4 tbsp olive oil
1 large carrot, cut into chunks
1 large onion, cut into chunks
2 celery sticks, roughly chopped
1 bottle red Burgundy
2 thyme sprigs
1 head of garlic, cut in half horizontally
4 bay leaves
1.5kg (3lb 5oz) chuck steak or blade steak, cut into 5cm (2in) cubes
55g (2oz) unsalted butter
225g (8oz) smoked streaky bacon or pancetta, cut into lardons
450g (1lb) shallots, peeled
2 tbsp plain flour
600ml (1 pint) fresh beef stock (from a carton is fine)
salt and freshly ground black pepper
350g (12oz) small chestnut mushrooms, trimmed
5 tbsp brandy

to garnish
roughly chopped flat-leaf parsley

to serve
purple-sprouting broccoli

1. Put 1 tbsp oil in a heavy-based saucepan over a medium heat. Add the carrot, onion and celery and cook for 2–3 minutes, stirring. Pour in the wine and stir in the thyme, garlic and 2 bay leaves. Bring to the boil, then reduce the heat and simmer, uncovered, for 15 minutes. Allow to cool completely.

2. Place the beef in a large non-metallic bowl and pour over the wine mixture. Cover with cling film and place in the fridge to marinate overnight.

3. Preheat the oven to 150°C/300°F/Gas 2. Place a colander over a large bowl, then strain the beef. Reserve the liquid marinade and set aside. Put 25g (1oz) butter and 1 tbsp oil in a large frying pan over a medium heat. Add the bacon and cook for 6–8 minutes, stirring occasionally, until sizzling and golden brown. Stir in the shallots and then transfer to a large casserole.

4. Put 1 tbsp oil in the same frying pan over a high heat. Pat dry the drained beef cubes with kitchen paper. Brown all over, in batches. Remove with a slotted spoon and transfer to the casserole with the bacon and shallots.

5. Add 2–3 large spoonfuls of the reserved marinade to the frying pan and allow to bubble, scraping the bottom of the pan with a wooden spoon to loosen any sediment. Pour into the casserole. Sprinkle over the flour and stir in the remaining marinade and bay leaves and the beef stock. Season generously and bring to the boil, then cover and place in the oven for 3–3½ hours, until the beef is cooked and very tender but still holding its shape.

6. About 50 minutes before the end of the cooking time, heat the remaining oil and butter in a frying pan and cook the mushrooms for 6–8 minutes until lightly browned. Add the brandy and cook for another few minutes, then stir into the casserole, replace the lid and return it to the oven for 30 minutes.

7. Remove the casserole from the oven and season to taste. Sprinkle with the parsley and serve with a bowl of steamed purple-sprouting broccoli.

To make this in a slow cooker
Make sure your slow cooker is large enough for all the ingredients. You will need to reduce both the wine and stock by about a third. Transfer the beef bourguignon to your slow cooker in step 5, once it is boiling. Cover and cook for on low for 6–8 hours until the meat is cooked. Add the mushroom mixture prepared in step 6 for the last hour of cooking.

This is one of our best-selling dishes at The Greyhound. I've made a couple of changes to the traditional recipe that I think enhance this classic: red peppers and gherkins. If you get a little delayed, don't worry, an extra half an hour or so will be fine, that's the beauty of slow cooking. Just top up with a little stock if needed, before you stir in the soured cream.

Paprika goulash

750g (1lb 10oz) onions, roughly chopped

25g (1oz) unsalted butter

1kg (2lb 4oz) chuck steak, brisket or silverside, cut into 4cm (1½in) cubes

55g (2oz) seasoned plain flour

125g (4½oz) pork belly or smoked streaky bacon, cut into 1cm (½in) cubes

3 garlic cloves, finely chopped

1 red pepper, cored, deseeded and cut into 1cm (½in) dice

2 tsp caraway seeds

2 tsp sweet paprika, plus extra for serving

600ml (1 pint) beef stock

2 tbsp tomato purée

1 tsp sea salt

freshly ground black pepper

300ml (½ pint) soured cream

2 tbsp chopped sour gherkins or cornichons

to serve

new potatoes

soured cream, mixed with chopped sour gherkins or cornichons

1. Put the onions in a food processor and blitz to a purée. Set aside.

2. Melt the butter in a heavy-based saucepan. Roll the beef in the seasoned flour and fry in the butter, over a high heat, until golden on all sides. Remove with a slotted spoon and set aside.

3. Add the pork belly to the same saucepan and brown all over, then add the garlic, red pepper, onion purée, caraway and paprika and cook over a medium heat for 3 minutes, stirring occasionally.

4. Return the beef to the pan and add the stock, tomato purée, salt and a few turns of black pepper. Bring to the boil, reduce the heat, cover and then simmer for 2 hours, stirring from time to time, until the meat is cooked.

5. Five minutes before the end of cooking, stir in the soured cream with the gherkins but do not allow to reboil. Serve with new potatoes, dolloped with some more soured cream mixed with chopped gherkins, and sprinkled with a little more paprika.

To make this in a slow cooker
Instead of cooking the goulash on the hob in step 4, transfer the mixture to the slow cooker when boiling, then cover and cook on low for 6–8 hours until the meat is cooked. Continue with step 5.

SERVES 4

PREP 30 MINS

COOKING 8–10 HRS

SETTING HIGH & LOW

I'm cheating a little here, and why not? It takes a couple of days
to make proper cassoulet, with all the stages. So this is not the real
McCoy, but it's delicious all the same.

Cassoulet in a day

4 duck legs

250g (9oz) pork belly, cut into
2.5cm (1in) chunks

1 onion, roughly chopped

250g (9oz) smoked Toulouse sausages,
thickly sliced, or raw garlic sausage,
skin removed, cut into 2.5cm (1in)
chunks

2 celery sticks, thinly sliced

4 garlic cloves, finely chopped

2 tbsp plain flour

400g (14oz) tin chopped tomatoes

2 tbsp tomato purée

3 thyme sprigs

2 bay leaves

½ tsp ground cloves

200ml (6½fl oz) dry white wine

250ml (8½fl oz) chicken stock

salt and freshly ground black pepper

2 x 400g (14oz) tins haricot or
cannellini beans, drained and rinsed

55g (2oz) fresh white breadcrumbs

to serve

green salad
crusty bread

1. Trim any excess fat from the duck legs and discard, then dry-fry in a large
frying pan over a low heat until the fat begins to run. Increase the heat and
brown the legs all over. Lift out and set aside. Add the diced pork belly and
onion and fry until lightly browned.

2. Stir in the sausage, celery and garlic, fry for 2 minutes, then mix in the
flour, tomatoes, tomato purée, herbs and cloves. Add the wine and stock
and bring to the boil. Season well.

3. Tip half the beans into the slow cooker. Add half the hot tomato mixture,
then arrange the duck over the top in a single layer. Cover with the
remaining beans and spread the remaining tomato mixture in an even layer
on top, then sprinkle with the breadcrumbs.

4. Cover and cook on high for 30 minutes, reduce the heat to low and cook
for 7½–9½ hours, until the breadcrumbs have absorbed the sauce and the
duck is cooked and almost falls off the bone when tested with a spoon.

5. Ladle into 4 warm shallow soup bowls.

SERVING SUGGESTION
A large bowl of salad and some crusty bread is all you need to accompany
this. Try tossing a few handfuls of watercress leaves, some dandelion or
rocket and some separated leaves of red-tinged endive with a dressing of
olive oil and sherry vinegar.

I think many people equate meatballs with a cheap meal, but why not make the most of them? I've gone down the Italian route, packing them with loads of flavour and accompanying them with a scrummy tomato sauce.

Pork, apple and lemon thyme meatballs

for the meatballs

1 slice of white bread

60ml (2fl oz) milk

500g (1lb 2oz) pork mince

1 Cox's apple, peeled, cored and grated

3 spring onions, finely chopped

55g (2oz) Kalamata olives, stoned and roughly chopped

40g (1½oz) Parmesan, grated

1 tbsp finely chopped lemon thyme leaves (or thyme or oregano)

1 tbsp runny honey

1 egg, beaten

1 garlic clove, crushed to a paste with a little sea salt

salt and freshly ground black pepper

1 tbsp olive oil

for the sauce

1 garlic clove, crushed to a paste with a little sea salt

1 red chilli, finely chopped

2 anchovy fillets in oil, chopped

1 onion, finely chopped

2 x 400g (14oz) tins chopped tomatoes

4 thyme sprigs

1 tbsp caster sugar

to serve

buttered fettuccine

grated zest of ½ unwaxed lemon

25g (1oz) Parmesan, grated

small basil leaves

1. Rip the bread into small pieces and soak it in the milk for 5 minutes. Squeeze some of the milk from the bread, then place the bread in the bowl with the remaining meatball ingredients. Mix well, season and then shape into golf-ball-sized balls.

2. Put the oil in a large frying pan over a high heat, then fry the meatballs until brown all over, remove to a plate and set aside.

3. Add the garlic, chilli, anchovy and onion to the pan and fry over a gentle heat for about 8 minutes to soften but not colour. Add the tomatoes, thyme and sugar, and simmer for 10 minutes, then season. Spoon the sauce into your slow cooker, then add the meatballs, toss gently to combine, cover and cook on low for 7–8 hours until the meatballs are cooked.

4. Serve on buttered fettuccine, and sprinkle with lemon zest, grated Parmesan and basil leaves.

To prepare in advance
You can make the meatballs in advance to save time, refrigerate overnight and then fry them in the morning before going to work.

The southern states of North America love big flavours and their version of paella lives up to expectations.

Mixed grain jambalaya

8 skinless chicken thigh fillets, halved

1 tbsp seasoned potato flour

1 tbsp vegetable oil

115g (4oz) raw garlic sausage, roughly chopped and lightly dry-fried

115g (4oz) chorizo sausage, roughly chopped and lightly dry-fried

1 onion, finely chopped

1 garlic clove, finely chopped

½ red pepper, cored, deseeded and cut into 1cm (½in) dice

½ green pepper, cored, deseeded and cut into 1cm (½in) dice

1 tsp soft thyme leaves

1 red chilli, deseeded and roughly chopped

200g (7oz) tin chopped tomatoes

500ml (18fl oz) chicken stock

55g (2oz) pearl barley, soaked in water for 30 minutes and drained

85g (3oz) brown basmati rice, rinsed

15g (½oz) millet seeds, dry-fried until they "pop"

8 raw jumbo prawns, peeled and deveined

25g (1oz) pumpkin seeds

115g (4oz) okra, thinly sliced

2 tbsp finely chopped flat-leaf parsley

salt and freshly ground black pepper

1. Dust the chicken in the potato flour. Put the oil in a large non-stick frying pan over a high heat, add the chicken and the dry-fried garlic and chorizo sausages and lightly brown, then remove and set aside.

2. Add the onion, garlic, peppers, thyme and chilli to the same pan and cook over a medium heat for 8 minutes, stirring continuously, to soften the onion. Place in the slow cooker with the meat.

3. Add the tomatoes and chicken stock. Cover and cook on low for about 5–8 hours, until the chicken is almost cooked.

4. Remove the lid and add the pearl barley, rice and millet, cover and cook for 1½ hours, until the chicken is thoroughly cooked and the grains tender. Turn the slow cooker to high, fold in the jumbo prawns, pumpkin seeds and okra, cover and cook for a further 40 minutes. Finally, fold in the parsley and season to taste.

To peel and devein prawns
Start at the large end and peel away the shell. To devein, cut a shallow slit down the middle of the outside curve of each prawn with a sharp, pointed knife. Pull out the dark vein, then rinse the cut under cold running water.

SERVES
4

PREP
20 MINS

MARINATE
1 HR

COOKING
6½–8½ HRS

SETTING
LOW &
HIGH

This is an unusual chicken dish inspired by a lovely lady from Trinidad, who taught me that you never chop up a Scotch bonnet chilli when cooking a stew, always leaving it whole so that you can fish it out when the dish has reached the required chilli heat.

Caribbean chicken stew

8 chicken thighs, skin on

juice of 1 lemon

1 tbsp salt

2 onions, roughly chopped

4 garlic cloves, roughly chopped

2 tsp soft thyme leaves

2 bay leaves

3 tbsp tomato ketchup

1 tbsp Worcestershire sauce

325g (11½oz) chicken livers, cleaned and halved

4 tbsp rapeseed or vegetable oil

4 tbsp Demerara sugar

450ml (¾ pint) chicken stock, hot

1 Scotch bonnet chilli, left whole

2 tbsp grated creamed coconut (from a solid block)

90ml (3fl oz) double cream

salt and freshly ground black pepper

to serve

steamed vegetables or rice

boiled potatoes

1. Place the chicken in a bowl. Mix with the lemon juice and salt. Leave for 5 minutes then rinse, drain and pat dry.

2. Place the onions, garlic, thyme, bay leaves, ketchup and Worcestershire sauce in a blender and process to a smooth paste.

3. Spoon half the paste over the chicken and toss to combine. Then do the same to the chicken livers. Leave both to marinate for 1 hour.

4. Split the oil and sugar between 2 frying pans over a medium heat, stir until the sugar dissolves and begins to caramelize. Continue to heat until deep golden. Wipe the marinade from the chicken and the livers. Add the chicken to one pan and the livers to the other. Stir both to coat with the caramel and cook for 2 minutes.

5. Place the chicken with the marinade and sugars in your slow cooker, pour on the stock, add the chilli cover and cook on low for 6–8 hours.

6. Increase the heat to high and add the chicken livers, grated coconut and cream, then stir to combine. Cook for 30–40 minutes, check the seasoning and remove the chilli.

7. Serve with steamed vegetables or rice, and boiled potatoes.

Simple country fare with a superb combination of flavours, which will be loved by all the family – it deserves a glass of cider or a fruity white wine.

Sausages, chicken, apples and plums

2 tbsp olive oil

450g (1lb) Toulouse or garlic sausages, cut into 1cm (½in) slices

8 chicken thighs, skin on

4 tbsp sherry vinegar

300ml (½ pint) chicken stock

150ml (¼ pint) dry white wine

2 bay leaves

4 sage leaves

2 thyme sprigs

16 plums or greengages, halved and stoned

8 garlic cloves, halved lengthways

2 large Granny Smith or Cox's apples, peeled, cored and cut into 2.5cm (1in) cubes

2 tbsp Dijon mustard

12 new potatoes, halved

25g (1oz) unsalted butter, diced

1 tbsp finely chopped mint

3 tbsp finely chopped flat-leaf parsley

salt and freshly ground black pepper

to serve
crusty bread
buttered cabbage

1. Heat the oil in a frying pan and brown the sausages and chicken in batches over a high heat. Remove with a slotted spoon and set aside.

2. Pour off most of the oil from the frying pan, add the vinegar and bring to the boil, scraping any sticky bits from the bottom and stirring together. Add the stock, wine, bay leaves, sage and thyme, then spoon into the slow cooker. Add the plums, garlic, apple, mustard, potatoes, sausages and chicken and stir to combine. Cover and cook on low for 7–8 hours until the meat is cooked.

3. Add the butter, mint and parsley, and swirl to combine. Taste and check the seasoning.

4. Serve with crusty bread and some buttered cabbage, if you like.

SERVES
4

PREP
20 MINS

COOKING
8 HRS

SETTING
LOW

Home-made baked beans by any other name. There are loads of flavours going into this dish, but they balance well by the end of the slow cooking. This is great as an accompaniment to grilled meat or fish, or just as a supper dish on its own with some toasted bread.

Chilli beans with chorizo and tomato

2 tbsp olive oil

450g (1lb) chorizo sausage, skin removed and cut into bite-sized chunks

115g (4oz) pancetta, diced

2 red onions, finely chopped

1 celery stick, finely chopped

1 large carrot, finely chopped

1 long mild red chilli, finely chopped

½ tsp dried chilli flakes

1 tsp smoked paprika

1 tsp dried oregano

2 tbsp tomato purée

2 x 400g (14oz) tins chopped tomatoes

400g (14oz) tin peeled cherry tomatoes

1 tbsp dark muscovado sugar

210ml (7fl oz) chicken stock, boiling or hot

2 x 400g (14oz) tins cannellini beans, drained and rinsed

salt and freshly ground black pepper

2 tbsp roughly chopped flat-leaf parsley

to serve

garlic-rubbed toasted ciabatta

1. Heat the oil in a large frying pan and cook the chorizo chunks over a medium heat for 5 minutes, stirring occasionally, to release the delicious paprika-flavoured fat. Remove the chorizo with a slotted spoon, leaving the fat behind, and set aside.

2. Cook the pancetta, onions, celery and carrot in the same pan over a medium heat for 8 minutes, to soften rather than colour. Add the chilli, paprika, oregano and tomato purée, stir to combine, then spoon into your slow cooker. Add the remaining ingredients, except the seasoning and parsley, cover and cook on low for 8 hours.

3. Check the seasoning, then stir in the parsley. Serve with garlic-rubbed toasted ciabatta.

Also try
Instead of the chorizo, try using your favourite pork sausage; just remove the skin, cut into chunks and cook in the same way.

SERVES 4 · PREP 30 MINS · COOKING 8–10 HRS · SETTING LOW & HIGH

Even if I say so myself, I make a mean chilli that had Lorraine Kelly on GMTV cooing appreciatively. Instead of using cocoa powder, you could grate in 25g (1oz) dark chocolate (more than 70% cocoa solids) just before serving. This idea has its roots in a Mexican *mole* (sauce), which often includes chocolate.

Chunky pork and beef chilli

60ml (2fl oz) olive oil

650g (1lb 7oz) stewing beef, cut into 1cm (½in) cubes

650g (1lb 7oz) shoulder of pork, cut into 1cm (½in) cubes

450g (1lb) smoked streaky bacon, diced

1.3kg (3lb) onions, finely chopped

2 tbsp finely chopped garlic

3 celery sticks, finely diced

5 mild red chillies, finely chopped

2 tbsp dried oregano

1 tbsp fennel seeds

2 tbsp ground cumin

2 tbsp paprika

1 tbsp ground coriander

2 tsp freshly ground black pepper

2 tsp ground cinnamon

1 tsp cayenne (to taste)

up to 900ml (1½ pints) beef stock, boiling or hot

2 x 400g (14oz) tins chopped tomatoes

2 bay leaves

1 tbsp cocoa powder (unsweetened)

3 tbsp tomato purée

2 x 400g (14oz) tins red kidney beans, drained and rinsed

salt and freshly ground black pepper

4 tbsp roughly chopped coriander leaves

1. Put the oil in a large frying pan over a high heat and brown the beef and pork all over, working in batches if necessary. Remove with a slotted spoon and place in your slow cooker.

2. In the same pan, cook the bacon, onions, garlic, celery and chillies in the oil for 8–10 minutes, stirring occasionally, until the bacon is golden brown. Add the dried oregano, fennel seeds and ground spices and cook for a further 2 minutes.

3. Add the bacon mix and half the stock to the slow cooker, then add the remaining ingredients, except the beans, seasoning and coriander and stir to combine. Cover and cook for on low for 6–8 hours, stirring occasionally, until the meat is cooked and tender.

4. Add the beans, making sure that they are covered, adding extra stock as required, turn the slow cooker to high, cover and cook for a further 2 hours, adding extra stock if necessary. Season to taste and fold in the coriander.

SERVING SUGGESTION
Serve with long-grain rice and any of the following garnishes: tortilla (soft or chips), guacamole, tomato salsa, finely sliced red onion, lime wedges, soured cream and grated Cheddar (Americans use Monterey Jack).

Reducing the sauce
If the sauce is too thin at the end of the cooking time, tip all the mixture into a large saucepan and boil vigorously until it has been reduced to the desired consistency.

SERVES
4

PREP
15 MINS

COOKING
4¼–6¼
HRS

SETTING
LOW &
HIGH

A bowl of this will nourish you in every way. It's a soup-cum-stew packed with flavour and very affordable. Vegetarians please feel free to remove the meat and substitute vegetable stock for the chicken. It's the barley that transports me straight back, across the years, to my grandmother and childhood.

Barley with greens, sausage and ham

115g (4oz) unsalted butter

2 onions, finely chopped

2 garlic cloves, finely chopped

½ tsp soft thyme leaves

2 handfuls mixed spring greens and rocket, roughly chopped

225g (8oz) pearl barley, rinsed and drained

55g (2oz) Parma or Serrano ham, finely chopped

½ tsp ground cayenne

900ml (1½ pints) chicken stock

2 handfuls baby spinach

55g (2oz) Parmesan, grated

4 tbsp chopped flat-leaf parsley

2 tbsp snipped chives

2 tbsp pine nuts, toasted

salt and freshly ground black pepper

115g (4oz) chorizo sausage, thinly sliced

1. Melt half the butter in a saucepan over a medium heat. Add the onions, garlic and thyme. Cook for 8 minutes, until the onions have started to soften but not colour. Transfer to your slow cooker.

2. Stir in the chopped greens, then fold in the barley, Parma ham, cayenne and chicken stock. Cover and cook on low for 4–6 hours.

3. Add the spinach, Parmesan, parsley, chives and pine nuts, stir to combine, then cover and cook on high for 15 minutes. Season to taste.

4. Just before the end of the cooking time, melt the remaining butter in a frying pan and cook the chorizo slices over a high heat, turning once, until browned and crisp on both sides.

5. Spoon the stew into 4 warm bowls and top with slices of crisp chorizo and a drizzle of the chorizo fat.

Curries & tagines

Red vegetable curry

see page 164

Chickpea and vegetable curry **158**

Ghugni **160**

Spiced vegetable dhal with coconut flavours **161**

Stewed artichoke tagine **162**

Red vegetable curry **164**

Kashmiri spiced vegetables **166**

Salmon in a spiced coconut cream **167**

Goan fish curry **168**

A pleasant little fish curry **170**

Smoked fish kedgeree **172**

Poached monkfish in spicy tomato sauce **174**

Sweet and spicy chicken wings **175**

Buttered chicken and tomato curry **176**

Chicken, Puy lentil and butternut curry **178**

Braised duck in red curry **180**

Kerala curried lamb shanks **182**

Beef rendang **183**

SERVES
4–6

PREP
30 MINS

COOKING
7–9 HRS

SETTING
LOW &
HIGH

A recipe that's not just for vegetarians. We should all be eating less meat and more vegetables, but if you're going to swap vegetables for meat, do put loads of flavour into the dish.

Chickpea and vegetable curry

2 large onions, roughly chopped

1 tbsp grated fresh ginger

4 tbsp good olive oil

1 tbsp finely chopped garlic

1 cinnamon stick

1 tsp ground turmeric

1 tsp garam masala

2 red chillies, finely sliced

400g (14oz) tin chopped tomatoes

2 crushed green cardamom pods

6 cloves

1 tsp black peppercorns

1 tsp toasted cumin seeds

200g (7oz) new potatoes, halved

½ cauliflower, broken into
   small florets

3 carrots, halved lengthways

400g (14oz) tin chickpeas, drained
   and rinsed

1 tbsp finely chopped mint

2 tbsp roughly chopped coriander
   leaves

250g (9oz) bag baby spinach, washed

salt and freshly ground black pepper

1. Blend half the onion and the ginger to a smooth paste in a mini food processor and set aside.

2. In a large frying pan, cook the remaining onion in the olive oil with the garlic and cinnamon over a medium heat for 8 minutes, until the onions have softened but not coloured. Spoon the mix into the slow cooker and add all the remaining ingredients except the fresh herbs and spinach. Cover and cook on low for 6–8 hours until the root vegetables are tender.

3. Turn the heat to high, fold in the mint, coriander and spinach and season to taste. Cover and cook for 1 hour. Serve immediately.

4. Serve with rice or as part of an Indian thali or buffet.

SERVES
4–6

PREP
25 MINS

COOKING
4–5 HRS

SETTING
LOW

Even the most ardent meat eater should try to eat more vegetarian food to improve their diet. So why not make the effort to create a curried chickpea dish packed full of delicious flavours. Rice and a cucumber and mint raita would be perfect accompaniments.

Ghugni

1 large bay leaf

5 green cardamom pods

3 cloves

2.5cm (1in) cinnamon stick

1 tsp each cumin and coriander seeds

60ml (2fl oz) vegetable oil

2 potatoes, cut into 2.5cm (1in) dice

½ fresh coconut, flesh finely sliced

1 large onion, finely chopped

1 tsp chilli powder

½ tsp fennel seeds, crushed

200g (7oz) tin chopped tomatoes

2 tsp ground turmeric

2 x 400g (14oz) tins chickpeas, drained
   and rinsed

450ml (¾ pint) vegetable stock

2 tbsp thick tamarind paste

1 tsp finely chopped garlic

2 tsp grated jaggery (palm sugar)
   or soft light brown sugar

pinch of salt

¼ tsp each ground cumin and chilli

to garnish

2.5cm (1in) piece of fresh ginger

2 medium green chillies, sliced

2 tbsp roughly chopped coriander

to serve

basmati rice

green salad

1. Dry-roast the bay leaf, cardamoms, cloves, cinnamon and the cumin and coriander seeds in a frying pan for 1–2 minutes, then grind to a fine powder in a mortar and pestle or electric coffee grinder.

2. Heat the oil in frying pan, then fry the diced potato over a medium heat until light golden brown. Add the coconut and onion to the pan and fry until just turning light brown. Spoon into your slow cooker.

3. Add the chilli powder, spice mix, fennel seeds, tomatoes, turmeric, chickpeas and stock. Stir to combine, cover and cook on low for 4–5 hours.

4. Near the end of the cooking time, mix the tamarind with 1 tbsp hot water, the garlic, jaggery, salt, cumin and chilli powder. When the jaggery has melted, drizzle this on top of the curried chickpeas.

5. For the garnish, slice the fresh ginger into very thin strips, then fry until crisp. Scatter over the ghugni with the sliced green chillies and coriander.

6. Serve with basmati rice and a herby green salad.

SERVES
4

PREP
15 MINS

COOKING
3¾–4¾
HRS

SETTING
LOW

This is a lentil dish to die for. I even love it at room temperature as part of an antipasti buffet. It's not at all difficult to make, and the spices turn the lentils golden.

Spiced vegetable dhal with coconut flavours

2 tbsp vegetable oil

2 medium onions, grated

4 garlic cloves, crushed to a paste with a little sea salt

1 carrot, finely diced

1 celery stick, finely diced

2 tsp ground cumin

1 tsp ground coriander

½ tsp ground fennel

2 tsp black or yellow mustard seeds

2 tsp ground turmeric

1 tsp chilli powder

1 tsp grated fresh ginger

225g (8oz) split red lentils, rinsed and drained

300ml (½ pint) vegetable stock, boiling

200g (7oz) tin chopped tomatoes

400ml (13½fl oz) coconut milk

1 bunch coriander, roughly chopped

juice and grated zest of 1 unwaxed or organic lemon

1 tsp garam masala

115g (4oz) French beans, topped, tailed and cut into 1cm (½in) pieces

25g (1oz) coconut flakes or desiccated coconut

1. Heat the oil in a frying pan, then cook the onions, garlic, carrot and celery over a medium heat for 6–8 minutes, stirring occasionally, until the vegetables are starting to soften but not colour.

2. Add the spices and ginger and cook for 2 minutes. Transfer the mixture to your slow cooker, then add the lentils, stock, tomatoes and coconut milk, and stir to combine. Cover and cook on low for 3–4 hours, stirring once.

3. Remove the lid and fold in the coriander, lemon juice and zest, garam masala and French beans. Cook, uncovered, for 40 minutes. Sprinkle with coconut flakes, which you could toast if you wish.

SERVES 4

PREP 25 MINS

COOKING 6¼–8¼ HRS

SETTING LOW & HIGH

Are artichokes worth the hassle? Only you can be the judge of that. I love them and with all the flavours going on here you've got yourself one hell of a vegetarian dish, so if you're unsure, try them.

Stewed artichoke tagine

juice of 1 lemon

4 large globe artichokes

2 garlic cloves, roughly chopped

10 black peppercorns, crushed

12 coriander seeds, toasted and crushed

¼ tsp ground turmeric

pinch of ground cayenne

¼ tsp toasted cumin seeds

2 onions, cut vertically into eighths

2 bay leaves

60ml (2fl oz) extra-virgin olive oil

pinch of saffron strands, soaked in 2 tbsp cold water

2 carrots, thinly sliced

300ml (½ pint) vegetable stock

8 dried apricots, thinly sliced

55g (2oz) raisins

25g (1oz) flaked almonds

400g (14oz) tin chickpeas, drained and rinsed

225g (8oz) baby spinach

2 tbsp roughly chopped coriander

4 tbsp roughly chopped flat-leaf parsley

salt and freshly ground black pepper

to serve

couscous or long-grain rice

1. Fill a large bowl with cold water and add the lemon juice. Trim each artichoke by peeling the stem until all the woody matter has disappeared. Pull off the tough outer leaves until you reach the pale green ones. Cut about 2.5cm (1in) off the top of each artichoke. Cut the artichokes vertically into 4, then cut or pull out the choke (the hairy bit in the middle) and discard. Rub all the cut surfaces with the squeezed lemon pieces and place the prepared artichokes in the bowl of water.

2. In a mortar and pestle (or electric coffee grinder) crush to a powder the garlic, peppercorns, coriander seeds, turmeric, cayenne and cumin.

3. Cook the onions and bay leaves in a frying pan with the olive oil, over a medium heat, for about 8 minutes, until soft but not coloured. Add the spice mix and cook for a further 3 minutes. Stir to combine.

4. Add the artichokes and the saffron with its soaking liquor, and toss to combine. Add the carrots, half the vegetable stock, apricots, raisins and almonds and stir to combine. Cover and cook on low for about 6–8 hours.

5. When the artichokes are tender, add the chickpeas, spinach, coriander and parsley, and stir to combine. Turn to high, cover and cook for 15 minutes.

6. Season to taste. Serve hot or cold with steamed couscous or rice.

SERVES
4

PREP
40 MINS

COOKING
4¼–6¼
HRS

SETTING
LOW &
HIGH

This recipe has its roots in Thailand, where red curry is a national favourite. It's cheap to make and very filling and nutritious.

Red vegetable curry

400ml (13½fl oz) tin coconut milk

100ml (3½fl oz) vegetable stock

2 carrots, diced

1 large onion, roughly chopped

8 garlic cloves, sliced

1 red pepper, cored, deseeded and roughly diced

100g (3½oz) sweet potato, cut into 2.5cm (1in) chunks

½ pumpkin or butternut squash, peeled, deseeded and cut into 2.5cm (1in) chunks

100g (3½oz) French beans, topped and tailed

2 courgettes, cut into 2.5cm (1in) discs

115g (4oz) frozen petits pois, defrosted

1 bunch spring onions, finely chopped

3 tbsp roughly chopped coriander

1 tbsp lime juice

1 tbsp Thai fish sauce (nam pla)

salt and freshly ground black pepper

for the curry paste

10 black peppercorns

2 tsp each cumin and coriander seeds

10 mild red chillies, deseeded

5 shallots, finely chopped

2 garlic cloves, crushed

2cm (¾in) piece of fresh ginger, chopped

6 lemongrass stalks, tough outer leaves removed, roughly chopped

grated zest of 1 lime

pinch of ground cinnamon

½ tsp ground turmeric

1 tbsp caster sugar

½ tsp salt

splash each of vegetable and chilli oil

1. To make the curry paste: fry the peppercorns and the cumin and coriander seeds until fragrant in a dry frying pan over a medium heat, then grind them to a powder in a mortar and pestle or electric coffee grinder.

2. Put this powder and all the other curry paste ingredients, except the oils, into a food processor and blend until smooth (it takes a good 5–10 minutes), adding a splash of water as necessary to help the process.

3. Warm the oils in a frying pan and add 4 good dessertspoonfuls of paste. Cook on a low heat until it becomes fragrant, stir to combine, then add to your slow cooker with the coconut milk, stock, carrots, onion, garlic, red pepper, sweet potato and pumpkin. Cover and cook on low for 4–6 hours.

4. Add the French beans, courgettes, peas and spring onions. Cook, uncovered, on high for 15 minutes. Fold in the coriander, lime juice and Thai fish sauce, and season to taste.

5. Garnish with sliced green chillies, lime wedges or halves and coriander leaves, and serve with steamed basmati rice.

SERVES
4–5

PREP
20 MINS

COOKING
7–9 HRS

SETTING
LOW &
HIGH

If I were vegetarian, I would get the majority of my diet from the Indian subcontinent and the Far East where delicious things are done to vegetables, so much so, that meat and fish could become a distant memory. Again, despite the length of the ingredient list, this is a very straightforward recipe.

Kashmiri spiced vegetables

2 tsp cumin seeds, toasted

1 tsp coriander seeds, toasted

1 tsp fennel seeds

seeds from 2 green cardamom pods and 1 black cardamom pod (optional)

½ tsp ground cinnamon

3 garlic cloves, crushed to a paste with a little sea salt

½ tsp ground black pepper

½ tsp salt

1 tsp grated fresh ginger

1 tsp chilli powder

½ tsp ground turmeric

2 tbsp vegetable oil

1 onion, roughly chopped

2 large floury potatoes, cubed

1 sweet potato, cubed

1 small cauliflower, broken into florets

200g (7oz) tin chopped tomatoes

300ml (½ pint) vegetable stock

150ml (¼ pint) Greek yoghurt

175g (6oz) frozen peas, defrosted

2 handfuls baby spinach

1 tbsp coriander leaves

2 mild green chillies, deseeded and thinly sliced

2 ripe tomatoes, each cut into 6 wedges

25g (1oz) toasted flaked almonds

to serve

basmati rice

1. Put the cumin seeds, coriander seeds, fennel seeds and cardamom seeds in an electric coffee grinder, or mortar and pestle, and grind to a fine powder. Then mix with the cinnamon, garlic, black pepper, salt, ginger, chilli and turmeric.

2. Meanwhile, heat the oil in a frying pan and cook the onion over a medium heat for about 6–8 minutes until soft but without much colour. Then add the spice paste, mix well and cook for a further 2 minutes. Transfer to your slow cooker with the potatoes, cauliflower, tomatoes, stock and yoghurt, then stir to combine. Cover and cook on low for 6–8 hours.

3. Increase the setting to high, remove the lid, then fold in the peas, spinach, coriander leaves, green chillies and fresh tomatoes, then cook, uncovered, for 1 hour.

4. Scatter the almonds over the top and serve with basmati rice.

SERVES
4

PREP
25 MINS

COOKING
3½ HRS

SETTING
LOW &
HIGH

Salmon can be a bit bland and needs a little something to pep it up. But then again, salmon is a perfect fish for taking on powerful flavours.

Salmon in a spiced coconut cream

2 tbsp rapeseed or vegetable oil

1 onion, finely chopped

2 lemongrass stalks, tough outer leaves removed, roughly chopped

2 fresh kaffir lime leaves, centre stalks removed

3 garlic cloves, roughly chopped

4cm (1½in) piece of fresh ginger, finely sliced

1 tsp ground coriander

3 tbsp finely chopped coriander stalks and leaves

1 tsp chilli powder

1 tsp ground turmeric

210ml (7fl oz) coconut milk

200g (7oz) tin pineapple pulp in juice, drained

4 x 175g (6oz) skinless salmon fillets

1 tbsp Thai fish sauce (nam pla)

2 tbsp lime juice

salt and freshly ground black pepper

to garnish

2 spring onions, finely sliced

2 green chillies, deseeded and finely sliced

1 tbsp coriander leaves

to serve

basmati rice

1. Place 1 tbsp oil in a food processor with the onion, lemongrass, lime leaves, garlic, ginger, ground coriander, chopped coriander, chilli powder and turmeric. Blend until fairly smooth.

2. In a frying pan, heat the remaining oil and gently cook the spice paste for 2–3 minutes, not allowing it to colour too much. Spoon this mixture into your slow cooker, then add the coconut milk and pineapple pulp. Cover and cook on low for 2 hours.

3. Add the salmon, replace the lid and continue to cook on low for 1 hour, then increase the setting to high and cook, uncovered, for 30 minutes. Remove the salmon steaks to a warm dish, cover loosely with foil and keep warm.

4. Fold the Thai fish sauce and lime juice into the spiced coconut sauce and season to taste. Spoon over the salmon, then scatter with the spring onions, sliced chillies and coriander leaves. Serve with rice.

Pineapple pulp
If you can't find pineapple pulp, just blend some tinned or fresh pineapple to a pulp instead.

SERVES
4–6

PREP
30 MINS

MARINATE
20 MINS

COOKING
1½ HRS

SETTING
LOW

When I first started writing this book, my initial thought was
why slow-cook fish when it's usually a very fast supper? What
I discovered, however, is that the flavours are intensified and,
because of the nature of the cooking, the fish doesn't fall apart.

Goan fish curry

3 tbsp coconut milk

55g (2oz) tamarind paste, mixed with
2 tbsp water

1 tbsp runny honey

½ tsp salt

1kg (2lb 4oz) pollack fillets (left
whole), skin on

1 tbsp Thai fish sauce (nam pla)

for the curry paste
115g (4oz) desiccated coconut

10–12 black peppercorns

2 tsp dried chilli flakes

1 tbsp ground coriander

10–12 garlic cloves, peeled

1 tbsp sesame seeds

3cm (1¼in) piece of fresh ginger,
roughly chopped

for the tempering
3 tbsp vegetable oil

2 tbsp black mustard seeds

8–10 curry leaves

3 green chillies, slit lengthways,
deseeded and thinly sliced

to serve
basmati rice

1. Combine the coconut milk with the tamarind paste, half the honey and
the salt, then add the fish, cover and marinate for 20 minutes. Drain and set
aside, retaining the marinade.

2. In a food processor, blend together all the ingredients for the curry paste
until smooth, adding a little marinade to facilitate the blending. Add the
remaining marinade. Pour the mixture into your slow cooker and add the
remaining honey, the Thai fish sauce and the fish pieces. Cover and cook on
low for 1½ hours.

3. Heat the oil in a frying pan and add the mustard seeds, curry leaves and
green chillies. Cook on a high heat, stirring continuously to prevent burning.
When the chillies are flecked with brown, add the mixture to the curry.

4. Serve with rice.

Antony's tip
In Goa they use pomfret, but it's hard to find here, so do use any other
firm-fleshed white fish such as cod or monkfish. Get the fishmonger to
fillet the fish for you.

SERVES
4

PREP
20 MINS

COOKING
2¾ HRS

SETTING
LOW &
HIGH

A curry influence works wonders on good white fish and slow cooking works a treat too. If you want to add a selection of green vegetables to bulk up the curry, add them at the same time as the fish.

A pleasant little fish curry

2 tbsp rapeseed or vegetable oil

1 onion, finely chopped

1 garlic clove, crushed to a paste with a little sea salt

1 tsp grated fresh ginger

1 tsp ground cardamom

1 tsp ground coriander

½ tsp ground cumin

½ tsp ground fennel

1 tsp chilli powder

1 tsp ground turmeric

½ tsp English mustard powder

300ml (½ pint) coconut milk

200g (7oz) tin chopped tomatoes

675g (1½lb) skinless firm white fish fillets (eg monkfish, halibut, turbot), cut into 2.5cm (1in) dice

salt and freshly ground black pepper

to garnish

tomato, deseeded and diced

coriander leaves

to serve

basmati rice

1. Heat the oil in a heavy-based saucepan or frying pan over a moderate heat. Add the onion, garlic and ginger and cook for 8 minutes, until the onion is soft but not coloured.

2. Meanwhile, mix the spices with 2 tbsp water to create a smooth paste, then fold into the softened onion and cook gently for a further 2 minutes, stirring regularly.

3. Transfer this mix to your slow cooker, pour in the coconut milk and tomatoes, give it a little stir, cover and cook on low for 2 hours.

4. Fold in the fish and cook, uncovered, on high for 45 minutes, until the fish is cooked through.

5. Season to taste, garnish with the diced tomato and coriander leaves and serve with rice.

I'm a massive fan of kedgeree, a colonial dish from Britain's days in India where it was usually served at breakfast dish. I've made it healthier by adding a good oily fish, mackerel.

Smoked fish kedgeree

250g (9oz) skinless undyed smoked haddock fillets cut into 2cm (¾in) pieces

1 onion, finely sliced

1 leek, finely shredded

40g (1½oz) unsalted butter

2 tsp mild curry paste

1 tsp ground turmeric

2 bay leaves

225g (8oz) easy-cook basmati rice, rinsed and drained

2 sachets dashi powder or 1 fish stock cube, crushed

3 tbsp double cream

1 smoked mackerel fillet, skinned and flaked

1 hot-smoked salmon fillet, flaked

3 hard-boiled eggs, roughly chopped

1 tbsp snipped chives

2 plum tomatoes, deseeded and cut into small dice

1 tbsp finely chopped flat-leaf parsley

to serve

leafy salad

1. Pour boiling water over the smoked haddock and allow to sit for 10 minutes. Drain.

2. Meanwhile, in a frying pan, cook the onion and leek gently in the butter for 6–8 minutes, until the onion has softened but not coloured. Fold in the curry paste, turmeric and bay leaves, stir to combine, then fold in the rice and stir to coat.

3. Transfer the rice mixture to your slow cooker and add 600ml (1 pint) boiling water with the dashi powder or stock cube. Stir to combine, then cover and cook on low for 2–3 hours, until the rice is tender and the liquid has been absorbed.

4. Fold in the haddock and the remaining ingredients, cover and cook on high for 20 minutes. Serve with a well-dressed leafy salad.

SERVES
4

PREP
15 MINS

COOKING
4½ HRS

SETTING
LOW &
HIGH

Monkfish is the perfect fish for the slow cooker as it's meaty, has no bones and stays intact. It may be expensive, but see this as a dish for entertaining that's well worth the expense.

Poached monkfish in spicy tomato sauce

1 tbsp rapeseed or vegetable oil

1 onion, grated

4 garlic cloves, crushed to a paste with a little sea salt

2 red chillies, deseeded and finely sliced

½ tsp chilli powder

½ tsp ground turmeric

½ tsp ground cumin

½ tsp ground coriander

½ tsp ground fennel

2 green cardamom pods, crushed

150ml (¼ pint) passata

60ml (2fl oz) fish or chicken stock

400g (14oz) tin cannellini beans, drained and rinsed

juice of 2 limes

700g (1lb 9oz) monkfish fillet, cut into 4 steaks

175g (6oz) frozen peas, defrosted

1 tsp garam masala

1 tsp finely chopped mint

3 tbsp roughly chopped coriander

salt and freshly ground black pepper

to serve
Greek yoghurt
basmati rice

1. Heat the oil in a frying pan and gently cook the onion, garlic and chillies for 8 minutes, until the onion is soft but not coloured. Add all the spices, except the garam masala, and cook for 1 minute, stirring to combine.

2. Transfer the onion mix to your slow cooker. Stir in the passata, stock, cannellini beans and lime juice. Cover and cook on low for 2½ hours.

3. Add the fish fillets to the slow cooker with the peas. Increase the heat to high, cover and cook for 1½ hours.

4. Lift the fish carefully from the sauce to a warmed dish and cover loosely with foil to keep warm.

5. Fold the garam masala and herbs into the sauce and cook, uncovered, for 20 minutes.

6. Season to taste, then spoon the spicy sauce over the fish. Top each portion with a dollop of yoghurt and serve with rice.

SERVES 4–6 | PREP 20 MINS | MARINATE 4 HRS | COOKING 6–7 HRS | SETTING LOW

There are so many recipes for chicken wings, but I reckon this is my favourite. Give it a go and see what you think.

Sweet and spicy chicken wings

1 tbsp Szechwan peppercorns, toasted and ground

1 tbsp grated garlic

3 tbsp grated fresh ginger

4 tbsp grated orange zest,

4 spring onions, cut into 2.5cm (1in) pieces

1 red chilli, finely chopped

2 tbsp runny honey

2 tbsp soy sauce

90ml (3fl oz) corn oil

30ml (1fl oz) sesame oil

1kg (2lb 4oz) chicken wings, cut in half through the joint, tips discarded

salt and freshly ground black pepper

450ml (¾ pint) peach nectar

to garnish

2 tbsp finely chopped parsley

2 tbsp snipped chives

1. In a mini blender or mortar and pestle, blend the peppercorns, garlic, ginger, 3 tbsp orange zest, spring onions and chilli until you have a rough paste.

2. In a large bowl, combine the honey, soy sauce and oils with the paste and toss with the chicken wings. Season to taste. Cover with cling film and leave to marinate for at least 4 hours, or preferably overnight, in the fridge.

3. Remove the chicken from the marinade and cook in a frying pan over a high heat, turning once, until the chicken is golden brown, then place in your slow cooker with the marinade and peach nectar. Cover and cook on low for 6–7 hours until the meat is cooked through.

4. Garnish with a mixture of the remaining orange zest, the chopped parsley and chives, and serve on its own as a snack or with rice.

Also try
You can also use drumsticks instead of chicken wings. The cooking time is exactly the same.

Zesting oranges
1 orange should produce 1 tbsp grated zest. Use organic oranges if available.

Buttered chicken is a classic mild curry. It has loads of ingredients, but they are all widely available, so don't be put off because it's well worth making. You'll see I've used chicken thighs because I feel they give a sweet result, but if breasts are your thing, go for it.

Buttered chicken and tomato curry

1kg (2lb 4oz) skinless chicken thigh fillets, halved

2 tbsp lemon juice

½ tsp salt

1 tsp chilli powder

300ml (½ pint) Greek yoghurt

2 tsp ground ginger

2 tsp garam masala

115g (4oz) unsalted butter

1 tbsp vegetable oil

2 onions, finely chopped

4 garlic cloves, crushed to a paste

1 tsp ground coriander

½ tsp each ground cumin and fennel

1 tsp sweet paprika

400ml (13½fl oz) passata

2 tbsp tomato purée

150ml (¼ pint) chicken stock

2 tbsp grated jaggery (palm sugar)

1 cinnamon stick, broken in half

3 tomatoes, roughly chopped

90ml (3fl oz) double cream

salt and freshly ground black pepper

to garnish
coriander leaves
flaked almonds
spring onions, sliced
85g (3oz) feta or paneer cheese

to serve
basmati or pilau rice

1. Place the chicken in a non-metallic bowl and toss with the lemon juice, salt and chilli powder. Cover and marinate, ideally for 3–4 hours in the fridge, but at least 30 minutes.

2. Whisk together the yoghurt, ginger and half the garam masala, pour over the marinated chicken and mix well. Spoon the chicken mix into the slow cooker.

3. Heat one-third of the butter with the oil in a frying pan over a low heat, then cook the onion with the garlic and spices for 8 minutes, until the onion has softened but has not much colour. Stir the onion mix into the chicken, then stir in the tomato passata, tomato purée, stock, jaggery and cinnamon. Fold into the chicken mix, pop on the lid and cook on low for 5–6 hours, until the chicken is cooked through.

4. Fold in the remaining garam masala, fresh tomatoes and cream, then cover and cook on high for 20 minutes.

5. Remove the chicken to a warm serving dish, then whisk the remaining butter into the sauce, making sure it is well emulsified. Check the seasoning, then pour the sauce over the chicken and garnish with coriander leaves, almonds and spring onions. Just before serving, grate the cheese over the surface. Serve with basmati or pilau rice.

Palm sugar
If you can't find jaggery or palm sugar, use soft light brown sugar.

Don't panic about the number of ingredients – if you're into curries you should have all the spices in your larder or cupboard. What you have here is a genuine curry with two lentils, one of which stays intact while the other should start to break down.

Chicken, Puy lentil and butternut curry

2 tbsp rapeseed or vegetable oil

2 onions, finely chopped

3 garlic cloves, crushed to a paste with a little sea salt

2 tsp grated fresh ginger

1 tsp ground cumin

1 tsp ground fennel

1½ tsp ground coriander

1 tsp black mustard seeds

1 tsp chilli powder

1 tsp ground turmeric

1 litre (1¾ pints) good chicken stock

900g (2lb) skinless chicken thigh fillets, halved

400g (14oz) tin chopped tomatoes

1 medium butternut squash, peeled, deseeded and cut into bite-sized pieces

400ml (13½fl oz) coconut milk

140g (5oz) Puy lentils, rinsed and drained

140g (5oz) red lentils, rinsed and drained

2 tomatoes, cut into rough chunks

175g (6oz) frozen peas, defrosted

salt and freshly ground black pepper

to garnish

red chillies, finely sliced

coriander, roughly chopped

mint, finely chopped

to serve

basmati rice

1. Heat the oil in a large frying pan over a medium heat and cook the onion, garlic and ginger for 8 minutes, until the onion has softened but has not much colour. Add all the spices and cook for a further 5 minutes.

2. Add the stock and bring to the boil, then pour the mix into the slow cooker and add the chicken, tinned tomatoes, butternut squash, half the coconut milk and lentils. Stir to combine. Cover with the lid and cook on low for 7–8 hours until the chicken is cooked through.

3. Add the remaining coconut milk, fresh tomatoes and peas, stir to combine, and cook, uncovered, on high for 25 minutes. Season to taste and garnish with the chillies, coriander and mint. Serve with rice.

SERVES
4

PREP
20 MINS

COOKING
8¼ HRS

SETTING
LOW &
HIGH

I was taught this dish in the Oriental Thai Cooking School in Bangkok, which was superb even if a little painful for the bank balance. You could use a whole duck and get your butcher to portion it, but I use duck legs because they are so much cheaper. This works very well with chicken and pork too.

Braised duck in red curry

6 duck legs, cut into 2.5cm (1in) pieces (bone in) by a butcher

2 tbsp duck fat or vegetable oil

12 shallots, thinly sliced

6 garlic cloves, finely chopped

2 tbsp grated fresh ginger

75g (2¾oz) Thai red curry paste

400ml (13½fl oz) tin coconut milk

1 tbsp soft light brown sugar

3 fresh kaffir lime leaves, thinly sliced

2 tbsp lime juice

20 basil leaves, ripped

3 handfuls spinach

1 tbsp Thai fish sauce (nam pla)

to garnish

1 bunch coriander, leaves only

1 bunch spring onions, thinly sliced

2 green chillies, deseeded and thinly sliced

to serve

Thai fragrant rice

1. Brown the duck pieces in a frying pan with the duck fat over a high heat. Remove and set aside. Add the shallots and garlic to the pan and cook over a medium heat for about 8–10 minutes, until the shallots start to brown, stirring from time to time.

2. Add the ginger and curry paste and cook for 3 minutes, stirring continuously. Put the duck in your slow cooker and add the contents of the frying pan, coconut milk, sugar and lime leaves. Cover and cook on low for 8 hours, until the duck is cooked through and tender.

3. Add the lime juice, basil leaves, spinach and Thai fish sauce, stir to combine, then cook, uncovered, on high for 15 minutes.

4. Garnish with the coriander leaves, spring onions and chillies, and serve with Thai fragrant rice.

My friend Merrilees Parker introduced me to a version of this curry after her travels in India. I've changed it a fair bit to reflect my taste, but it's a delicious change from kleftiko or braised lamb shanks with rosemary and garlic.

Kerala curried lamb shanks

90ml (3fl oz) rapeseed or vegetable oil

6 green cardamom pods, lightly crushed

1 cinnamon stick, broken in half

2 star anise, broken into small pieces

1 tsp cumin seeds

½ tsp coriander seeds

½ tsp fennel seeds

2 onions, finely chopped

5cm (2in) piece of fresh ginger, roughly chopped

6 large medium-hot green chillies, roughly chopped

½ tsp chilli powder

2 tsp ground turmeric

2 x 400g (14oz) tins chopped tomatoes

1 tbsp tomato purée

1 tbsp grated jaggery (palm sugar) or soft light brown sugar

210ml (7fl oz) chicken stock

210ml (7fl oz) coconut cream

4 lamb shanks, soaked in cold water for 30 minutes and drained

to serve

basmati rice

1. Heat the oil in a frying pan. Add the cardamom, cinnamon, star anise and cumin, coriander and fennel seeds and cook for 2 minutes over a gentle heat until fragrant. Remove and set aside, leaving the oil in the frying pan.

2. Meanwhile, in a food processor, blend together the onions, ginger, chillies, chilli powder and turmeric to make a smooth paste. Spoon this paste into the spiced oil and fry gently for 8 minutes, until lightly browned. Put this mixture and the cooked spices, tomatoes, tomato purée, jaggery, stock and coconut cream into your slow cooker.

3. Place the lamb shanks in the curry sauce. Cover and cook on low for 8–10 hours until the meat is cooked and almost falling off the bone. Remove the shanks gently to a serving dish, then skim off the majority of the fat from the surface of the sauce.

4. Pour the sauce over the shanks and serve with basmati rice.

SERVES **4** · PREP **30 MINS** · COOKING **2½–3 HRS** · HOB

Slow cooking doesn't just mean European flavours, as this superb "dry" curry from Malaysia illustrates. If making in a slow cooker, the sauce will be wetter, as there will not be the same evaporation, but none the less delicious.

Beef rendang

2 tbsp vegetable oil

6 green cardamom pods, crushed

1 cinnamon stick, broken in half

650g (1lb 7oz) braising or stewing steak, cut into 5cm (2in) cubes

400ml (13½fl oz) coconut milk

6 kaffir lime leaves, fresh or dried

grated zest of 2 organic limes

300ml (½ pint) beef stock

55g (2oz) desiccated coconut

2 tbsp tamarind paste or juice of 2 limes

2 tbsp finely chopped coriander

for the rendang paste

2 onions, roughly chopped

4cm (1½in) piece of fresh ginger, chopped

1 tbsp roughly chopped galangal (or another tsp roughly chopped ginger)

4 garlic cloves

2 lemongrass stalks, tough outer leaves removed, roughly chopped

2 tsp ground turmeric

6 long dried red chillies, soaked in water for 30 minutes and drained

to garnish

coriander sprigs

lime cheeks (slice either side of core)

to serve

basmati rice

1. First make the rendang paste: place all the ingredients in a food processor and blend to a smooth paste.

2. Heat a frying pan and add the oil. Fry the paste over a high heat for about 3 minutes until it darkens and is aromatic. Add the crushed cardamom pods and cinnamon and cook for another minute.

3. Add the beef and fry it in the paste, stirring all the time, until it is well sealed.

4. Pour over the coconut milk and bring to a gentle simmer. Add the kaffir lime leaves and lime zest. Season with salt and stir well. Cook very gently for 2½–3 hours, uncovered, stirring frequently. Top up with stock if the sauce gets too dry. The meat should be really tender and cooked through, and the sauce greatly reduced and almost dry.

5. Meanwhile, toast the coconut in a dry pan, taking care as it burns easily. Blitz to a powder in a small blender or electric coffee grinder, or use a mortar and pestle. When the rendang is ready, stir the coconut into the curry with the tamarind paste or lime juice and the chopped coriander.

6. Garnish with a few sprigs of coriander and lime cheeks and serve immediately with basmati rice.

To make this in a slow cooker
Reduce the amount of stock by half. In step 4 cover and cook for 6–8 hours on low, then turn the slow cooker to high and cook for 1½ hours. Top up with hot stock if the sauce gets too dry.

Puddings
&
treats

Baked chocolate custard cups

see page 192

A chocolate saucy pudding **188**

Chocolate-baked cheesecake with a brownie twist **190**

Baked chocolate custard cups **192**

Rich maple crème caramel **194**

Marmalade-brioche baked custard **196**

Treacle sponge **197**

Baked Lebanese fruit with melting blue cheese **198**

Spiced apple terrine and honeyed yoghurt **200**

Baked fruit and nut apples **202**

Poached quince with vanilla yoghurt mousse **204**

Jamaican coconut bananas **205**

Poached figs with blackberries **206**

Compote of pears, prunes, oranges and walnuts in spiced wine **208**

Braised pear with Roquefort **210**

Spiced carrot cake with cream cheese frosting **212**

A Christmas quantity of classic mincemeat **214**

A pleasant lemon curd **215**

SERVES 4 | PREP 15 MINS | COOKING 2½–3 HRS | SETTING HIGH

A classic that has stood the test of time and that I'm sure has been produced in many a household. It's a must with your slow cooker!

A chocolate saucy pudding

85g (3oz) unsalted butter, plus extra for greasing
180ml (6fl oz) milk
1 tsp vanilla extract
225g (8oz) caster sugar
1 egg, beaten
225g (8oz) self-raising flour
½ tsp baking powder
4 tbsp good cocoa powder
225g (8oz) soft light brown sugar
600ml (1 pint) boiling water

1. Lightly grease your slow cooker bowl.

2. Melt the butter in the milk over a low heat. Remove from the heat and whisk in the vanilla extract and caster sugar, until the sugar has dissolved. Stir in the egg.

3. Sift together the flour, baking powder and 2 tbsp cocoa, and fold into the milk mixture.

4. Spoon the mixture over the bottom of the cooker bowl and level the surface, then evenly sift the brown sugar and the remaining cocoa over the top. Gently pour the boiling water over the sugared batter, cover and cook on high for 2½–3 hours until the centre is firm. Remove the bowl from the cooker and allow to stand for 10 minutes before serving.

SERVING SUGGESTION
This is good with cream or ice-cream or both, but beware, it's not to be eaten on a regular basis!

MAKES 9

PREP 30 MINS + REFRIGERATE 1 HR

COOKING 2¼ HRS

SETTING HIGH

The brownie is one of our best-selling puddings at both The Greyhound and our deli, Windsor Larder. By adding the cheesecake topping, this is a great marriage of two hugely popular puddings.

Chocolate-baked cheesecake with a brownie twist

85g (3oz) dark chocolate (70% cocoa solids), roughly chopped

85g (3oz) unsalted butter, roughly diced

10g (3¾oz) caster sugar

2 eggs, beaten

40g (1½oz) plain flour

½ tsp baking powder

40g (1½oz) milk chocolate buttons or milk chocolate cut into small chunks

40g (1½oz) white chocolate buttons or white chocolate cut into small chunks

40g (1½oz) pecans (optional)

2 tbsp mini marshmallows

for the cheesecake topping

175g (6oz) full-fat cream cheese

40g (1½oz) caster sugar

1 tsp vanilla extract

1 egg, beaten

to serve

vanilla ice-cream

1. Line the base and sides of a 15cm (6in) square cake tin with lightly greased baking (parchment) paper.

2. Pour 7cm (2¾in) hot water into the ceramic slow cooker bowl and turn to high. Put an upturned saucer or plate in the bottom of the slow cooker. Place the dark chocolate and butter in a heatproof bowl, put in the slow cooker and leave for about 10 minutes until the chocolate has melted. Remove the bowl from the slow cooker.

3. Meanwhile, make the cheesecake topping by beating together the cream cheese, caster sugar and vanilla extract. Then gradually whisk the egg into the mix until it's very smooth.

4. Stir the chocolate and butter together until smooth and velvety, then whisk in the sugar. Gradually beat in the egg until combined (it may look as if it's splitting, but have no fear). Sift the flour and baking powder over the mix and carefully fold them in with the chocolate buttons and nuts, if using. Spoon the mix into your cake tin, level the surface and dot with the mini marshmallows.

5. Dollop small spoonfuls of cheesecake topping onto the surface of the chocolate mix and then, using a fork, swirl the cheesecake and brownie mixtures together to get a marbled effect.

6. Cover the cake tin with foil, then place on the upturned saucer in the bottom of the slow cooker. Pour in more boiling water to just over halfway up the sides of the cake tin, cover and cook on high for 2¼ hours, until almost set in the centre. Cool the cake in the tin on a rack.

7. Turn out and refrigerate for at least 1 hour, then cut into 9 squares. Serve with vanilla ice-cream.

SERVES
6

PREP
20 MINS

COOKING
2 HRS
4.5 L
LARGE POT

SETTING
HIGH

**What could be nicer than baked custard with chocolate magic –
a classic French concept. It's equally good served hot or cold as
a mousse, and it can be made well in advance.**

Baked chocolate
custard cups

500ml (18fl oz) double cream

250ml (8½fl oz) full-fat milk

1 vanilla pod, split lengthways and
seeds scraped out

2 tbsp good cocoa powder

175g (6oz) dark chocolate (more than
55% cocoa solids), finely chopped

2 eggs

4 egg yolks

115g (4oz) caster sugar

to serve

cream

good cocoa powder, for dusting

1. Place the cream, milk, vanilla pod and seeds, cocoa powder and dark chocolate in a saucepan over a medium heat and bring to the boil to melt the chocolate, stirring from time to time. Remove from the heat and set aside.

2. Place the eggs and yolks with the sugar in a bowl and whisk until pale and ribboning. Gradually add the chocolate cream and whisk well to combine. Strain the chocolate custard into 6 teacups or ramekins, place in the slow cooker and carefully pour boiling water around them to come halfway up the sides. Cover and cook on high for 2 hours, until set.

3. Remove from the water bath and allow to cool for 5 minutes before serving. Dust with cocoa powder and serve with cream.

Also try
For a more adult taste, add a couple of shots of liqueur – Kahlúa, coffee or chocolate – when heating the cream mixture.

I learned this recipe in California. It's a cross between crème caramel and crème brûlée but without its sugar topping. The maple syrup gives it a delicious flavour, enhanced by the lovely runny caramel.

Rich maple crème caramel

300g (10½oz) caster sugar
500ml (18fl oz) double cream
100ml (3½fl oz) full-fat milk
120ml (4fl oz) pure maple syrup
2 eggs
6 egg yolks

1. Make a caramel by gently dissolving the sugar in 100ml (3½fl oz) water in a small heavy-based saucepan, then boil without stirring until the syrup turns a golden colour (but do not allow it to darken or it will be bitter).

2. Pour the hot caramel into 6 x 150ml (¼ pint) dariole moulds, working quickly. Tilt each mould to ensure it is evenly lined on the bottom and a little way up the side with caramel, discard any excess and allow the caramel to cool.

3. Bring the cream, milk and maple syrup to simmering point in a saucepan over a medium heat. Whisk the eggs and egg yolks in a bowl, then slowly pour in the hot cream, whisking continuously. Pour the cream mix through a fine-mesh sieve into a jug, then carefully fill the prepared moulds. Remove any surface bubbles using a teaspoon.

4. Place the moulds in the slow cooker. Pour in boiling water to come three-quarters of the way up their sides, cover and cook on low for 3–3½ hours.

5. Remove the lid and allow the creams to cool in the slow cooker, then take them out of the water, place on a tray and cover in cling film. Refrigerate for at least 5 hours before serving.

Make this in advance
This pudding can be made up to 2 days in advance.

SERVES 4

PREP 40 MINS

SOAK 30 MINS

COOKING 3–4 HRS

SETTING HIGH

This is a posh bread-and-butter pudding using that lovely eggy brioche instead of leftover bread. The slow cooker produces excellent results with a perfect custard finish.

Marmalade-brioche baked custard

350g (12oz) brioche, cut to the shape of the terrine and into 1cm (½in) slices to fit

115g (4oz) unsalted butter, softened, plus extra for greasing

350g (12oz) orange marmalade

1 litre (1¾ pints) double cream

500ml (18fl oz) full-fat milk

1 vanilla pod, split lengthways and seeds scraped out

juice and grated zest of 1 organic orange

90ml (3fl oz) Cointreau or Grand Marnier

4 eggs

6 egg yolks

225g (8oz) caster sugar, plus extra for sprinkling

to serve

ice-cream or vanilla custard

1. Lightly butter a 1kg (2lb 4oz) terrine. Spread the brioche slices with the butter, then the marmalade, and arrange overlapping in several layers in the terrine. Place the cream, milk and vanilla pod and seeds into a saucepan and bring to the boil, then remove from the heat and set aside.

2. Put the orange juice and zest, liqueur, eggs, egg yolks and sugar into a large bowl and whisk until well combined. Then pour over the cream mixture, whisking continuously until smooth. Strain this custard over the brioche, then sprinkle with a little caster sugar to coat the surface. Leave the brioche to soak up the custard for 30 minutes.

3. Place the terrine in the slow cooker and carefully pour boiling water around it to come halfway up the sides. Cover and cook on high for 3–4 hours, until just set.

4. Remove from the slow cooker and allow to rest for 15 minutes before serving with ice-cream or vanilla custard.

SERVING SUGGESTION
If you wish, you can scatter the surface of the cooked pud with a thin layer of caster sugar and glaze with a blowtorch or under a very hot grill.

Also try
Thinly slice a peeled organic orange and arrange the orange between the slices of brioche when layering the pudding.

SERVES
6–8

PREP
20 MINS

COOKING
3¼–4
HRS

SETTING
HIGH

This brings back memories of childhood. Every day we would indulge in a hot pudding and this was one of my favourites. Gone are the days of 2 hours' exercise every day, so puddings have become a rare treat for me.

Treacle sponge

3 tbsp golden syrup

175g (6oz) unsalted butter, plus extra for greasing

1 tbsp fresh white breadcrumbs

juice of 1½ lemons

175g (6oz) caster sugar

grated zest of 1 unwaxed or organic lemon

3 eggs, beaten

200g (7oz) self-raising flour

about 3 tbsp milk

to serve
custard or cream

1. Place the golden syrup in a buttered 1.2 litre (2 pint) pudding basin with the breadcrumbs and juice of ½ lemon.

2. To make the sponge: place the butter and sugar in a bowl and gently cream together until pale, using an electric whisk. Mix in the lemon rind and then slowly whisk in alternate spoonfuls of beaten egg and flour until both have been used up. Fold in the remainder of the lemon juice and just enough milk for the mixture to drop easily from the spoon.

3. Spoon the sponge mixture over the syrup in the pudding basin. Cover with a circle of greaseproof paper, pleated in the centre to allow room for expansion while cooking. Place a double piece of buttered foil on top and secure with string, making a handle so that you can easily lift the basin.

4. Place the pudding on an upturned plate or saucer inside your slow cooker, and pour in enough boiling water to come two-thirds up the side of the basin. Cover and cook on high for 3¼–4 hours, until a skewer comes out clean. Occasionally, as the water evaporates, top up with boiling water.

5. Remove the pudding basin from the slow cooker and allow to cool slightly. Cut away the string and remove the foil and greaseproof paper. Invert the treacle sponge onto a serving plate, ensuring that all the syrup comes out from the bottom of the basin. Serve with custard or cream.

SERVES
6

PREP
20 MINS

SOAK
30 MINS

COOKING
2½ HRS

SETTING
HIGH

This is a sophisticated pudding and a little unusual. A cross between savoury and sweet, the dried fruit marries well with my favourite blue cheese, which is made locally to me, near Reading.

Baked Lebanese fruit with melting blue cheese

40g (1½oz) unsalted butter, melted, plus extra for greasing

150g (5½oz) dried figs, roughly chopped

150g (5½oz) dried apricots, cut into 0.5cm (¼in) dice

100g (3½oz) Medjool dates, sliced

55g (2oz) dried cherries

40g (1½oz) dried blueberries

25g (1oz) dried mixed peel

180ml (6fl oz) Orange Muscat or sweet wine

180ml (6fl oz) water

½ tsp ground cinnamon

55g (2oz) semolina

2 tsp runny honey

½ tsp orange flower water

175g (6oz) Barkham Blue cheese, (or other blue cheese) thinly sliced

1. Lightly butter 6 x 150ml (¼ pint) dariole moulds (small enough to fit into your slow cooker) and place in the fridge for the butter to set hard.

2. Mix together the dried fruit and the Orange Muscat and leave to soak for 30 minutes, stirring from time to time.

3. Add all the other ingredients except the cheese. Stir to combine. Fill each mould three-quarters full with the pudding mix.

4. Place the moulds in the bottom of your slow cooker and then carefully pour hot water around them to come halfway up the sides. Cover and cook on high for 2½ hours until the puddings are set.

5. Turn out the puddings onto a baking tray and top each with a slice or 2 of blue cheese. Place under a hot grill, and when the cheese has melted, serve immediately.

Slow cooking this unusual apple terrine is perfect for developing the natural appley flavours. I've used Cox's and my favourite Bramley apples, but feel free to play with whatever apple grabs your fancy.

Spiced apple terrine and honeyed yoghurt

175g (6oz) caster sugar

750g (1lb 10oz) Cox's apples, peeled and cored

750g (1lb 10oz) Bramley apples, peeled and cored

grated zest of 1 unwaxed or organic lemon

grated zest of 1 organic orange

2 tsp ground cinnamon

½ tsp ground star anise

55g (2oz) flaked almonds, toasted

240ml (8fl oz) Greek yoghurt

1 tbsp runny honey

1. Line a 21cm x 8cm x 9cm (1lb) terrine or loaf tin – or similar – with a layer of foil and a layer of baking (parchment) paper, allowing a 10cm (4in) overhang on the long sides.

2. Combine half the sugar with 3 tbsp water in a small heavy-based saucepan over a medium heat, allow the sugar to dissolve completely, then swirl around gently for another 6–8 minutes until the sugar has turned a pale golden colour (but do not allow it to darken or it will be bitter). Pour the caramel into the base of the terrine and allow to cool.

3. Meanwhile, thinly slice the apples and toss with the zests. Mix the remaining sugar with the cinnamon and star anise, then toss with the apple and almonds.

4. Layer the apple mix on top of the caramel in the terrine. Cover the apple mix with the parchment and foil, then wrap the whole terrine in another layer of foil to enclose completely.

5. Place in the slow cooker and carefully pour boiling water into the slow cooker bowl to come halfway up the sides of the terrine. Cover with a lid and cook on low for 8 hours. Cool, weight to compact the terrine and refrigerate overnight.

6. Combine the yoghurt and honey, and refrigerate until needed.

7. To serve, gently tip the terrine onto a platter, remove the wrappings and carefully cut into 2.5cm (1in) slices using a serrated or, ideally, an electric carving knife. Serve with the honeyed yoghurt.

Make this in advance
You can make the terrine at least 24 hours ahead – it will keep for 1 week.

SERVES 4 · PREP 15 MINS · COOKING 4 HRS · SETTING HIGH & LOW

Let's hear it for the Bramley, the UK's very own cooking apple, which is, in my opinion, the star of this category of apple. With slow cooking you won't have the problem of bursting apples.

Baked fruit and nut apples

85g (3oz) unsalted butter, at room temperature

90ml (3fl oz) cranberry juice

4 large Bramley apples, cored

100g (3½oz) dark muscovado sugar

grated zest and juice of 1 organic orange

grated zest of 1 unwaxed or organic lemon

¼ tsp apple pie spice

3 tbsp well-crushed amaretti biscuits

40g (1½oz) macadamia nuts, roughly chopped

25g (1oz) dried cranberries

1 tbsp mincemeat (see page 214)

2 tbsp amaretto liqueur

to serve
clotted cream or custard

1. Grease the slow-cooker ceramic pot with a quarter of the butter, then pour in the cranberry juice, cover and turn the cooker to high.

2. With a melon baller or teaspoon, enlarge the apple cavity to twice its size. Run the tip of a sharp knife skin deep around the circumference of each apple.

3. Put the remaining butter, sugar, citrus zests and juice, spice and biscuits in a bowl and mulch together with a wooden spoon. Then add all the remaining ingredients, except the apples.

4. Divide the mixture between the apples, filling the cavities completely and piling any excess on top and under the apples. Stand the apples upright in the slow cooker, cover and reduce the temperature to low, then cook for 4 hours, until the apples are tender.

5. Transfer the apples to 4 warm bowls with any excess filling and the juices. Serve with clotted cream or custard.

Apple pie spice
If you can't find apple pie spice in the shops, combine 1 tbsp ground cinnamon, ½ tsp grated nutmeg, 1 tsp ground allspice and ¼ tsp ground cloves. It will keep for months in an airtight jar.

SERVES
4

PREP
45 MINS

COOKING
8¼–10¼
HRS

SETTING
LOW

Quince is a fruit you rarely see on sale in the greengrocer and never in the supermarket, but as it is such a delicious fruit, it's well worth making a detour to find in autumn. Shaped like a very hard yellow pear, it takes a lot of cooking, but it does have a magical perfume and flavour that isn't found anywhere else.

Poached quince with vanilla yoghurt mousse

for the poached quince

500g (1lb 2oz) caster sugar

300ml (½ pint) Marsala or sweet sherry

½ vanilla pod, split lengthways

½ cinnamon stick

½ tsp mixed spice

1 bay leaf

1 thyme sprig

2 large quinces

1 strip of unwaxed or organic orange rind

for the yoghurt mousse

2 gelatine leaves

420ml (14fl oz) double cream

85g (3oz) caster sugar

1 vanilla pod, split lengthways

300ml (½ pint) Greek yoghurt

1. To poach the quinces, first place the sugar, 1.2 litres (2 pint) water, Marsala, spices, bay leaf and thyme in a saucepan and bring to a gentle boil. Simmer for 5 minutes, until the sugar has dissolved and the liquid is clear.

2. Peel and halve the quinces, retaining the peel. Pour the poaching liquid into your slow cooker with the orange rind, quince halves and peel. Ensure the quinces are covered with liquid – add a layer of wet crumpled greaseproof to keep the fruit submerged – cover and cook on low for 8–10 hours until the fruit is tender, topping up with boiling water as necessary.

3. Meanwhile, to make the mousse, soak the gelatine in cold water for 8 minutes without stirring. Drain.

4. Gently heat half the cream with the sugar and vanilla pod in a saucepan to just under boiling, stirring to dissolve the sugar. Remove from the heat and stir in the gelatine to melt. Allow to cool (but not get cold or the gelatine will set), then strain through a sieve into a bowl.

5. Fold in the yoghurt and whisk to emulsify. Whisk the remaining cream until ribboning, then fold into the yoghurt mix. Refrigerate until needed.

6. Remove the cooked quinces from the poaching liquor, then cut out the core from the centre of each quince half.

7. Strain the poaching liquor into a saucepan and boil over a fierce heat for 10–12 minutes, until it becomes a sticky syrup. Allow the syrup to cool to room temperature.

8. Place a quince half in each bowl, spoon a dollop of mousse into its centre and drizzle over a little spiced syrup.

The more I go to Jamaica, the more I'm inspired by their simple use of indigenous ingredients. The freshest of fish, the wonderful jerk (traditional spice rub for meat) and perfectly ripened tropical fruit. Here I'm using Britain's most popular fruit, the banana.

Jamaican coconut bananas

55g (2 oz) Californian sultanas
90ml (3fl oz) dark rum
120ml (4fl oz) coconut milk
55g (2oz) unsalted butter, diced
85g (3oz) dark muscovado sugar
4 yellow (but not overripe) bananas, peeled and halved lengthways
pinch of grated nutmeg
pinch of ground allspice
90ml (3fl oz) double cream
25g (1oz) fresh coconut flakes

to serve
rum and raisin ice-cream

1. Soak the sultanas in the rum for 30 minutes.

2. Place the coconut milk, butter, sugar, sultanas and rum in the slow cooker on high and leave, uncovered, for 30 minutes, until the butter and sugar have melted, then stir to combine.

3. Add the bananas, cover and cook on high for 40 minutes, turning the bananas once. Sprinkle with the spices, add the cream and stir to combine. Cover and cook for a further 20 minutes.

4. Carefully lift the bananas onto 4 warm plates. Spoon over the sauce and sprinkle with the coconut flakes. Serve hot with rum and raisin ice-cream.

SERVING SUGGESTION
Toast the coconut flakes, if you like, in a dry frying pan over a medium heat, until just turning brown, but beware they burn easily. Some supermarkets sell prepared, ready-peeled fresh coconut, so you could create your own flakes with a potato peeler.

Lucky man that I am, I have a fig tree … in Spain. And I've discovered that figs work a treat in my slow cooker and don't show much sign of shrinkage.

Poached figs with blackberries

300g (10½oz) blackberries, defrosted
  if frozen
juice of 1 orange
juice of 2 lemons
115g (4oz) caster sugar
2 tbsp crème de cassis (optional)
12 fresh figs

to decorate
a few mint leaves (optional)

to serve
250ml (8½fl oz) crème fraîche
2 tbsp finely chopped mint
1 tbsp runny honey

1. Purée the blackberries with the orange juice in a food processor or liquidizer until smooth, then press through a sieve and discard the seeds. Gently heat the lemon juice and sugar in a small saucepan, stirring until the sugar has dissolved.

2. Stir the blackberry purée and cassis, if using, into the lemon syrup, then pour into the slow cooker. Add the figs, cover and cook on low for 2–3 hours.

3. Meanwhile, mix the crème fraîche with the chopped mint and honey and spoon into a small serving bowl. Refrigerate until needed.

4. Serve the figs while still warm or transfer to a glass dish and chill. Sprinkle with extra mint leaves, if you like, and serve with spoonfuls of the crème fraîche.

Also try
Halved peaches with a raspberry Melba sauce would also be great cooked this way.

You could also try stirring a little chopped stem ginger into the crème fraîche instead of the mint and honey.

SERVES
4

PREP
25 MINS +
REFRIGERATE
3 HRS

COOKING
3–4 HRS

SETTING
LOW

You've got a double whammy here: a perfect breakfast dish or a grown-up pud.
If you're not a fan of prunes (and there are many who remember the suffering at
school), just leave them out or substitute some other dried fruit.

Compote of pears, prunes, oranges and walnuts in spiced wine

4 Conference pears, peeled and halved
with the stems left intact

2 organic oranges

8 Agen prunes

16 walnut halves

for the spiced wine

450ml (¾ pint) red Beaujolais

115g (4oz) caster sugar

6 black peppercorns

pinch of grated nutmeg

pinch of ground cinnamon

½ tsp coriander seeds, toasted

1 clove

2 bay leaves

½ vanilla pod, slit lengthways

pared rind and juice of ½ organic
orange

juice of ½ lemon

2 tbsp redcurrant jelly

2 thin slices of fresh ginger

to serve

vanilla ice-cream (optional)

1. Combine all the ingredients for the spiced wine in a saucepan and bring just to the boil. Remove and keep warm over the lowest heat.

2. Remove the cores from the pears using a teaspoon or melon baller, then nestle them closely together in the base of the slow cooker. Pour the wine mixture over the top, making sure that the pears are submerged as much as possible using a layer of crumpled wet greaseproof paper. Cover and cook on low for 3–4 hours until the pears are tender.

3. Lift the pears out of the wine and transfer to a glass dish. Peel and de-pith the oranges, then slice each one into 6 horizontally, removing any pips. Add to the pears with the prunes and walnut halves.

4. Strain the wine mixture, if you like, over the pears. Leave to cool, then chill in the fridge for 3 hours. Serve on its own or with scoops of good vanilla ice-cream.

SERVING SUGGESTION
This tastes wonderful with home-made cinnamon ice-cream or try sprinkling bought vanilla ice-cream with a little ground cinnamon just before serving.

To make a thicker sauce
If you would like the spiced wine to be thicker, pour the liquid into a wide saucepan at the end of the pear cooking time. Boil rapidly for 5 minutes until reduced by about one-third, then pour over the pears and leave to cool.

SERVES
4

PREP
25 MINS

COOKING
1¾–2½
HRS

SETTING
HIGH

Blue cheese, pears, sweet wine and Roquefort – you just can't go wrong with this combo. It's great as a starter or even as a cheese course. Serve hot or at room temperature.

Braised pear with Roquefort

4 barely ripe Conference or Anjou pears, peeled, cored and halved vertically

55g (2oz) ricotta

55g (2oz) Roquefort

½ carrot, finely diced

½ celery stick, finely diced

4 Medjool dates, stoned and diced

1 tbsp runny honey

¼ tsp sweet paprika

150ml (¼ pint) sweet white wine (Orange Muscat or Beaumes de Venise)

freshly ground black pepper

pinch of grated nutmeg

pinch of ground cinnamon

5 tbsp finely chopped walnuts

to serve

salad leaves

225g (8oz) wedge of Roquefort

1. Place the pears, cut side up, on a chopping board. Hollow out a little of the centre of each with a teaspoon or melon baller.

2. Combine the ricotta, Roquefort, carrot, celery, dates, honey and paprika in a bowl. Spoon the mix into the pear cavities and place the pears, filling side up, in the base of the slow cooker.

3. Carefully pour the sweet wine around the pears and then sprinkle them with the pepper, nutmeg and cinnamon. Cover and cook on high for 1¾–2½ hours until the pears are tender.

4. Remove the pears carefully to a baking tray and place under a hot grill to brown.

5. Sprinkle with the walnuts and serve with some of the juices, dressed salad leaves and a wedge of Roquefort.

SERVES
8–10

PREP
40 MINS

COOKING
4–5 HRS

SETTING
HIGH

Carrot cakes are always a hit, but this one has a little more going on, with big flavours and lovely textures.

Spiced carrot cake with cream cheese frosting

unsalted butter, for greasing

325g (11½oz) self-raising flour

2 tsp baking powder

½ tbsp ground cinnamon

½ tsp grated nutmeg

½ tsp ground allspice

grated zest of 1 unwaxed orange

175g (6oz) soft dark brown sugar

180ml (6fl oz) olive oil

3 large eggs, lightly beaten

225g (8oz) cooked carrots, puréed

85g (3oz) carrot, grated

85g (3oz) walnuts, finely chopped

85g (3oz) raisins

55g (2oz) desiccated coconut

55g (2oz) tin crushed pineapple in juice, drained

for the cream cheese frosting

125g (4½oz) cream cheese or mascarpone

250g (9oz) icing sugar

90g (3¼oz) unsalted butter, softened

½ tsp vanilla extract

juice of ½ lemon

1. Line an 18cm (7in) round fixed-based cake tin with buttered greaseproof or baking (parchment) paper. Turn the slow cooker to high and pour in 2.5cm (1in) water. Put an upturned saucer or plate in the bottom of the slow cooker.

2. Sift together the flour, baking powder, cinnamon, nutmeg and allspice. Fold in the orange zest and brown sugar and combine well.

3. Add the oil, eggs, carrot purée, grated carrot, walnuts, raisins, coconut and pineapple to the dry ingredients and fold to combine, but don't overwork it.

4. Pour the mixture into the lined tin and level the surface. Place in the slow cooker and pour in more boiling water to come halfway up the sides of the tin. Cover and cook on high for 4–5, hours until the edge of the cake pulls away from the side of the tin, and a skewer inserted in the centre comes out clean.

5. Meanwhile, make the cream cheese frosting in a food processor. Blend all the ingredients together until smooth.

6. Remove the cake tin from the slow cooker and leave the cake to cool in the tin for 15 minutes, then turn out onto a cake rack, remove the baking paper and allow to cool completely.

7. Spread the cream cheese frosting on the top and side of the cake.

Choosing your tin
If you prefer, use a more traditional loaf or terrine tin, but make sure it's the same size as the one used in the recipe. The cooking time remains the same.

MAKES
2.5kg
(5½lb)

PREP
25 MINS

MARINATE
24 HRS

COOKING
3 HRS

SETTING
HIGH &
LOW

Why buy jars of bland mincemeat when it's so easy to make your own, and this one has the added thrill of proper booze. By slow cooking you lengthen the shelf life of the unopened product.

A Christmas quantity of classic mincemeat

200ml (6½fl oz) dark rum

270ml (9fl oz) dry sherry

500g (1lb 2oz) mixed currants, raisins and sultanas

500g (1lb 2oz) cooking apples, peeled, cored and finely chopped or coarsely grated

500g (1lb 2oz) shredded beef or vegetarian suet

100g (3½oz) flaked almonds, roughly chopped

115g (4oz) dried apricots, finely chopped

450g (1lb) light muscovado sugar

1 tsp ground cinnamon

pinch of grated nutmeg

1½ tsp mixed spice

grated zest and juice of 1 unwaxed or organic lemon

grated zest and juice of 1 organic orange

2 tsp ground ginger

200g (7oz) mixed candied peel, finely chopped

115g (4oz) glacé cherries, quartered

1. Mix half the rum and half the sherry in a large bowl with all the other ingredients, cover with cling film and leave for a day or so for the flavours to develop.

2. When ready, place the mincemeat in your slow cooker, cover and cook on high for 1 hour. Stir well. Reduce the heat to low, cover and cook for a further 2 hours, stirring halfway. Leave the mixture to cool completely, then fold in the remaining alcohol.

3. Pack the mincemeat into warm, sterilized jars (see opposite), and seal with waxed paper discs and tight-fitting lids.

4. The mincemeat will keep for up to 6 months in a cool, dry place, but once opened, store in the fridge for up to 4 weeks.

MAKES
500g
(1lb 2oz)

PREP
20 MINS

COOKING
2 HRS

SETTING
LOW

This is one of my favourite toast toppings, but it's not just a one-trick pony. Try lemon curd mixed with crumbled meringues and whipped cream; or meringue nests topped with whipped cream and a piping of lemon curd; or use it as a sponge cake filling.

A pleasant lemon curd

grated zest and juice of 3 unwaxed
  or organic lemons
115g (4oz) unsalted butter, diced
200g (7oz) caster sugar
2 large eggs and 2 yolks, beaten

1. Place the lemon zest and juice, butter and sugar in a non-stick saucepan and heat gently for 2–3 minutes, until the butter has melted, stirring from time to time. Pour into a bowl, then put this on an upturned saucer placed in the bottom of your slow cooker.

2. Strain the eggs and yolks through a sieve, add to the lemon mixture and stir well. Cover the bowl with foil (just pressed over the top), pour hot water to come halfway up the side of the bowl, cover and cook on low for 2 hours, until very thick. Stir once or twice during the cooking process.

3. Pour into small, warm, sterilized jars (see below), then cover the lemon curd with waxed discs and tight-fitting lids. Store in the fridge for up to 6 months.

How to sterilize jam jars
Sterilize jars by heating them in the oven at 150ºC/300ºF/Gas 2 for 20 minutes, then turn off the heat and allow the jars to cool slightly before potting the preserve. Alternatively, soak the jars in Milton solution, then rinse and put into the oven to dry out. I find it easiest to have all the jars on a tray and then, using a ladle, transfer the hot jam or curd into a jug before pouring it into the hot jars.

Stocks

MAKES
1.5 LITRES
(2½ PINTS)

PREP
15 MINS

COOKING
8–10 HRS

SETTING
HIGH

The perfect chicken stock

1 roast chicken carcass, chopped

500g (1lb 2oz) chicken wings, chopped

2 whole onions, spiked with 2 cloves
  each

1 carrot, thinly sliced

2 garlic cloves, crushed

1 celery stick, sliced

whites of 2 leeks, sliced

½ bunch of parsley, leaves and stalks

1 bouquet garni

½ bottle dry white wine

1 tsp white peppercorns, crushed

salt and freshly ground black pepper

1. Put the carcass and chicken wings in your slow cooker and add hot water to cover. Add all the remaining ingredients and cook on high, covered, for 8–10 hours, skimming every couple of hours. Add more water to top up if needed. Season to taste.

2. Strain through a fine sieve and leave to settle. Remove the fat, skimming off the last traces with kitchen paper.

3. Store in the fridge for up to 4 days or freeze (see tip opposite).

MAKES **500ml** (18FL OZ)

PREP **15** MINS

COOKING **8–10** HRS

SETTING **LOW**

The perfect vegetable stock

2 carrots, roughly chopped

2 onions, quartered

2 celery sticks, roughly chopped

½ fennel bulb, roughly chopped

2 leeks, roughly chopped

4 tomatoes, roughly chopped

8 button mushrooms, quartered

1 tsp black peppercorns

2 dried bay leaves

3 parsley stalks

2 thyme sprigs

1. Place all the ingredients in the slow cooker and cover with hot water. Cook on low for 8–10 hours. Strain into a large bowl and leave to cool.

2. Store in the fridge for up to 3 days or freeze (see below).

Freezing stock
To freeze, halve the stock by boiling it vigorously until it has reduced, then cool. Pour into ice-cube trays and freeze. When they have frozen, place the cubes into a labelled plastic freezer bag and use when required by placing in a jug and adding boiling water to dissolve.

Index

Acknowledgements

My great appreciation and fondness to Rebecca Spry for commissioning this book and for her good humour and tenacity throughout; an iron hand in a velvet glove.

Thanks also must go to Diona Murray, who diligently ploughed through my recipes, honed and gilded them; Elizabeth Zeschin who always does my recipes justice, one of the best food photographers around; Yasia Willams-Leedham and Juliette Norsworthy for putting together such a great design; and Georgina Atsiaris, my book editor, whose behind the scenes skills are always top-notch.

I must mention the constant support and encouragement of my brilliant wife, Jacinta and our children, Toby and Billie.

Finally, my thanks to Louise Townsend, my ultra-efficient PA, who was constantly on hand when the pressures of deadlines occasionally took their toll, and to Fiona Lindsay, my agent, and her team at Limelight Management, who provided their usual expertise and support.